GHOSTS
CAUGHT ON FILM

GHOSTS
CAUGHT ON FILM

PHOTOGRAPHS OF THE PARANORMAL

DR MELVYN WILLIN   FOREWORD BY PROF DONALD WEST

D&C
David and Charles

A DAVID & CHARLES BOOK
Copyright © David & Charles Limited 2007

David & Charles is an F+W Media Inc. company
4700 East Galbraith Road
Cincinnati, OH 45236

First published in 2007
Reprinted in 2008, 2009, 2010, 2011, 2012

Text copyright © Melvyn Willin 2007

Melvyn Willin has asserted his right to be identified as
author of this work in accordance with the Copyright,
Designs and Patents Act, 1988.

The publisher has endeavoured to contact all contributors
of pictures for permission to reproduce.

A catalogue record for this book is available from the
British Library.

ISBN-13: 978-0-7153-2728-9 hardback
ISBN-10: 0-7153-2728-3 hardback

Printed in Singapore by KHL Printing Co Pte Ltd
for David & Charles
Brunel House, Newton Abbot, Devon

Commissioning Editor: Neil Baber
Copy Editor: Glynn Christian
Assistant Editor: Louise Clark
Senior Designer: Sarah Clark
Production Controller: Kelly Smith

David & Charles publish high quality books on a
wide range of subjects.
For more great book ideas visit: www.rubooks.co.uk

Contents

Foreword

Melvyn Willin has amassed a unique and challenging collection of anomalous appearances on photographs. In this digital age of computer generated images one can scarcely conceive of an anomalous appearance on a photograph that could not be the result of artificial manipulation. Some of the examples here, however, are from an earlier era when it was easier to identify fraud. Covert manipulation of conventional cameras or of the developing process often left behind detectable traces of what had been done. Examples of this kind are scattered among this collection, and the methods that may have been used are explained in the commentaries.

Apart from deliberate fraud, some odd appearances may result from the accidental production of obscured or blurred shapes susceptible to being perceived by the eye of the beholder as a face or figure. The perception of an image as meaningful and recognizable is the end point of a process of integration and interpretation of sensory clues by complex neurological mechanisms that go on outside our conscious awarenenss. Where the clues are incomplete or ambiguous, the brain tends to fill in the gaps so that something familiar is seen that may not actually be there. Examples that may be due to th effect are also to be found here, especially among the instances of unexpected appearances occurring on snapshots.

The burning question is whether such mundane considerations can account for all cases, or whether there remain some instances where the camera has recorded a genuine phenomenon not visible to the persons present when the photo was taken. Melvyn is open minded about this, more so than many professional sceptics. He leaves readers to form their own judgements, but points out examples that are exceptionally puzzling, notably the Ted Serios pictures that were apparently imprinted on film by the power of thought alone. Except for the 'ectoplasmic' forms seen during séances, examples are very rare of an apparition seen by observers also being visible on a photograph taken at the time. One such, the Raynham Hall ghost, is included. It makes one eager to read up on the controversial results of investigations of the case that Melvyn cites.

A great deal of research has gone into finding the provenance of these pictures and outlining alternative theories about each one. The commentaries are learned and informative and communicated in Melvyn's inimitable, humorous style. One is left marvelling at the variety of attitudes and assumptions people bring to the subject and the changing ideas and fashions displayed in these photographs, ranging from faces of deceased relatives to ectoplasmic emanations, human auras and floating orbs. One can view the collection in different ways, as an historic documentary, a sociological study, a fascinating series of mysteries or a call for further research. It is frustrating that so many cases remain unsolved puzzles. Whether, like Melvyn, one does not dismiss the possibility of paranormal happenings, or whether one's only concern is the study of frauds and self-deceptions, this book provides much to think about. The Society for Psychical Research is fortunate to have an Honorary Archivist able to unearth so much interesting material.

Prof D.J. West
Professor Emeritus of Clinical Criminology

...actly what are ghosts? Are they really the elusive appearance of a dead person? Or does the human mind have the power to somehow project apparitions into the physical sphere? Perhaps they are a short-circuit in time, allowing us to glimpse the past; seeing a living person go about their business in their time, but appear as a ghost in ours. But ghosts are not necessarily visible, they may be spirits or the souls of the departed manifesting themselves as strange and unexplained lights, or in the activity of poltergeists randomly moving objects.

The problem, of course, is that the evidence is not conclusive. A photograph of a ghost is rarely claimed, although hauntings are relatively common. Strange noises, smells, changes in temperature and so on are often reported and some locations have won a considerable reputation for being haunted. However very few of the photographs in this book come from these places or from deliberate and planned photographing in a location where there have been ghost sightings. There are some famous exceptions, but by and large the photographs in existence that seem to defy any natural explanation have occurred by chance. Typically the photographer takes a routine photograph and later discovers that something strange had appeared on the film that was certainly not in frame when the shutter was pressed. When no obvious explanation seems to present itself, they seek the advice of experts (with many pictures in this book from the Society for Psychical Research). If the usual objections of multiple exposure, reflections and so on can be eliminated, then we are left with a mystery.

One could argue that the fact that the photographers had no special knowledge or interest in the paranormal means we should be a little less inclined to be sceptical about the circumstances of the pictures, there is no vested interest on their part as there might be with a ghost hunter or medium. But even if you can dismiss all but one of the photographs in this book as fake or mere coincidence, then that one is enough to allow the possibility that ghosts exist and may have been caught on film.

When I lecture in psychical research I always explain the basis for deciding what makes a photograph worth exhibiting and discussing. Not all of my chart of questions to establish veracity or mystery (next page) can be asked of every photograph, and only you will know the answers that are correct for you. Just as I find with my classes – and with me – the results are sometimes surprising. Yet every time you go through the process you will acquire a greater knowledge of your own strengths of belief and scepticism. That can only be a good thing. Here are some of the questions I ask:

- Is this photograph a deliberate fraud?
- Did an accidental flaw in photographic film or its development produce this image?
- Did the photographer knowingly use other people and/or props to achieve the images?
- Did the photographer forget or not notice other people in view at the time?
- Could the photograph be explained simply as the result of a repeatable or generally understood effect of light, or by an accidental intrusion in front of the lens?
- Does the photograph genuinely show an anomalous effect that is nonetheless within nature but not currently understood?
- Does the photograph genuinely show a paranormal effect that is outside nature as we understand it, and is thus beyond our comprehension?
- If I believe the photograph to illustrate something paranormal, does this strengthen my belief in religion, alien entities, or other psychical phenomena, or visa versa.
- Am I absolutely convinced that I have found the correct answer to the previous questions?

To those questions I should perhaps add the most obvious. What should a ghost look like? Sometimes you will be surprised to find a photograph published in this book which is accepted as being fraudulent. Such categorization will have been done well after it was first published. I show it to you because it illustrates what people thought was possible at the time. From its invention in the 19th century until well into the 20th century most people firmly believed the camera could not lie. They would have looked at these images quite differently from citizens of the 21st century, and it is educative for us to try to see them as they would.

Of course, you must expect my views to considerably influence my interpretations, and as well as that I point out opposite and suspicious views about the pictures, many of which are not of set-up séances but are what you'd call a 'snap'. Many of them have been sent to the Society for Psychical Research for help in understanding what has been captured and I am constantly impressed with the integrity and genuine esire people have to unravel the mysteries, usually without any preconceived ideas. It's now actually are for someone to stress the need for a paranormal interpretation at the expense of a natural one, whereas a century ago the reverse was more likely to be true.

Of course, there are many puzzling photographs which lie beyond the remit of this book. I decided to keep a focus on the human and allegedly human, such as ghosts and spirits. So, although the world of cryptozoology, which studies animals and creatures of uncertain origin that are believed to be extinct is fascinating, the world of the Loch Ness monster and the yeti will have to wait until another day. The same goes for the extraordinary genre of unidentified flying objects and the possibility of the existence of beings that live on the same time or space plane as us, but come from other planets and solar systems.

believe this book can be enjoyed in a number of different ways. It provides well researched information about many strange phenomena captured on film. Thus a serious investigator will find much that is new and with the references given at the end of the book pursue further enquiries. But the intriguing nature of the material surely means that it can be enjoyed by anyone, picked up and put down time after time, and form the basis of much discussion, even argument. There is nothing better a book can do.

Happy viewing and happy reading!

Dr Melvyn Willin
Honorary Archivist
Society for Psychical Research, London

THE EARLIEST IMAGES

The early days of photography (in the later 19th century up to the early part of the 20th century) could be called 'The Golden Age of the Medium'. Many of the photographs from this era are now known to have been faked, but were so sincerely believed to have been genuine at the time that they are of interest to us here. It was an age when belief in the afterlife was almost universal, and an unexpected windfall from the new invention of photography was that it seemed to prove this. Plangent hope of a life hereafter was given to mourners when their nearest and dearest appeared to return from the grave to be photographed in their company. The semitransparent look of these spirits was blamed not on willfully deceptive double exposure but on the insensitivity of camera film to the astral plane they inhabit when making earthly appearances. They were believed to mould themselves into their own likeness from profoundly mysterious ectoplasm, a vaporous substance, which supposedly emanated from the medium's body during a trance.

The most famous medium-photographers, such as Mumler (p.22), have generally been discredited but the legacy of their many surviving photographs demonstrates the widespread belief in this phenomenon across Europe and North America in the late 19th and early 20th centuries. Remember, at the time neither hypnotism nor photography was understood in the least by the general public. It was a time when almost everyone thought the camera could not lie. But it can. And now we would all accept that a crowd of onlookers who saw a person, animal, or bird emerge from what they were told was ectoplasm might well have been hypnotized, knowingly or not. Mass hypnotism is a fact, too.

Today we are less likely to accept the bird on Kluski's shoulder (p.20) is anything but real, of this world. The mystery to us is whether it was alive or dead, where it was before and where did it go after the séance? Some exponents might have been using rare forensic knowledge to exploit peculiarities of our eyes' behaviour. Remember, it is only because the eye retains an image for a split second that moving pictures and television were possible. Without knowing it

We all have the facility to join up still pictures into a sense of movement, if they are shown to us quickly enough. What else, unsuspected by their audience, might one of these early performers have known and exploited, perhaps about the performance of light itself? In the middle of the 20th century the idea of laser lights, pencil thin as they race miles in a straight line, would have been laughed at. Today they are an unremarkable part of everyday life.

The people who supported these early mediums by lending their, sometimes august, names are quite as fascinating as the mediums themselves. Sir William Crookes was one of the 19th century's most important scientists, doing work that led eventually to atomic theory. Was his life-long belief in the young medium Florence Cook based on the blind passion of an old fool for a young fool, or did he have to keep up his public face because it would have compromised his reputation as a scientist to admit he had quite literally been hoodwinked by cheap tricks? He could equally have been the only one who knew for sure her manifestations were genuine.

So, when you look at these remarkable photographs, look at them with two or three sets of eyes: eyes of the 19th, 20th, and 21st centuries. In the early 21st century few of us believe in fairies, and certainly not the winged dainties of the famous Cottingley photographs. Yet one hundred years ago most people thought that they just might be living at the bottom of someone's garden, maybe their own if only they knew how to see them. Sir Arthur Conan Doyle, creator of Sherlock Holmes, definitely believed and detected nothing fake about the dancing fairies who had been enticed to dance for the camera. The best reason for explaining why he didn't see the clues to the fraud is because he didn't want to do so. This could well be why these photographs were accepted when they were first published, but are now regarded with more wariness. Look at all these photographs through 19th, 20th or 21st century eyes, and whatever you see, I know you will find them quite as absorbing as I always do.

Did Silver Belle Materialize?

LOCATION: Camp Silver Belle, Ephrata, Pennsylvania, USA
DATE: probably between 1932 and 1961

Ralph Pressing, editor of *Psychic Observer*, was only two feet away, and part of an audience of 81 members when the ectoplasm of Silver Belle – the young Native-American spirit guide of Ethel Post-Parrish – gradually materialized. This infrared photograph is the second in a set of seven, and shows Ethel, a very well known medium, seated in the tent-like cabinet, itself the obvious origin of many chances to deceive.

The authenticity of this ectoplasm materialization has been challenged ever since the photograph was first published. Scoffers say these mysterious bodily effusions can be conjured using cheesecloth, and any layman who suspends disbelief will find anomalies. The fishtail of the apparition looks different and coincides too neatly with the side of the cabinet, the right side of which is suspiciously straight. Are those two feet at the bottom of the swirl? Why can we see wall details behind the woman holding back the curtain, but nothing behind the ectoplasm? It's even more interesting to speculate on the part infrared photography played. Infrared radiation makes human faces look dead white and with sunken eyes. But not here. Normal camera focusing can't always be used and filters – on to which anything might be painted – generally have to be attached. But infrared film uses normal developing techniques, and almost any illusion can be created.

'the young Native-American spirit guide of Ethel Post-Parrish, gradually materialized'

Yet, remember, this isn't an image that appeared only on film. Pressing and the audience believed they saw it, too. Protagonists counter this by saying that just because trained magicians can fake such effects it doesn't mean physical mediums are using such techniques, or not using mass hypnotism. Time to make up your own mind.

Faker, Fakir or Floater?

LOCATION: The Conway Hall, London, England
DATE: 1937 or 1938

For two years Colin Evans had audiences believing they were seeing the sort of miracle they'd only read about in the Bible, or that they had heard the holy Hindu fakirs of India could do, almost at will. The ability to levitate has been documented throughout history. Saints with the gift include Teresa of Avila, Francis of Assisi, and the mystic Joseph of Cupertino, affectionately known as 'The Little Friar Who Flew'. As soon as cameras existed there were pictures of Indian fakirs seeming to defy gravity by extreme body control, or trickery. The Society for Psychical Research even possesses old film footage of this Indian Rope Trick, and recent commentators now believe they can explain why it was an illusion. Even in the 21st century such stage magicians as David Copperfield and David Blaine appear to levitate, but no one today quite believes what they are seeing.

> 'using spiritual powers to defy Earth's natural laws'

This infrared photograph of Colin Evans was not thought to be a trick or illusion, but a factual record of him floating 15 feet above the ground, usually for about a minute. Contemporary scrutiny of the photograph has not been so kind. Sceptics point out the creasing of his trousers could indicate a cord attached to him, and then threaded through the audience and attached to a pulley system behind the door at the back of the hall. There's definitely something suspicious seeming to hang from his left-hand side. But why did none of his audiences ever suspect or say he was playing a trick? There were two further possible answers. Either he was a master of mass hypnotism, or he really was using spiritual powers to defy Earth's natural laws.

Do you Believe in Fairies?

LOCATION: Cottingley Glen, near Bingley, West Yorkshire, England
DATE: July 1917

Perhaps the most charming and inspirational of all allegedly paranormal pictures, the dancing fairies of Cottingley Glen, were believed in for decades. In fact they were championed by Sir Arthur Conan Doyle, creator of Sherlock Holmes and noted devotee of deductive logic. He embraced Spiritualism and, curiously, both his father and grandfather used to draw fairies as a pastime, so they were nothing new to him.

> 'an impressive recorded example of the paranormal'

In 1917 Elsie Wright, 15, and her cousin Frances Griffiths, 10, showed off a set of photographs of winged fairies they had enticed to dance for them. Doyle and the fairy 'expert' Edward L. Gardner were convinced by them but Sir Oliver Lodge of the Society for Psychical Research suspected fraud. Yet, thanks to Doyle's 1922 book, *The Coming of the Fairies*, the Cottingley Fairies became firmly lodged as an impressive recorded example of the paranormal. What they hadn't remembered was *Princess Mary's Gift Book* of 1915. In 1977 the writer Fred Gettings recognized the Cottingley Fairies were the same as those in that book. In late 1981 and early 1982, Elsie and Frances were interviewed by researcher Joe Cooper for the magazine *The Unexplained*, and finally admitted their sixty-year trickery. Frances also confessed all in a 1983 article in *The Times*. Between 1982 and 1983 the *British Journal of Photography* published articles revealing the cut-outs had been held in place by hat pins, which close scrutiny should have observed. Then, in 1995, the conjurer James Randi pointed out the small waterfall behind the fairies was considerably blurred because of the exposure time, but the fairies' supposedly fluttering wings were in sharp focus. Yet none of these revelations have stopped some people still believing in fairies, as you probably know yourself.

Suspicious Spirit Séance

LOCATION: Mornington Road, London, England
DATE: May 1874

When this very famous photograph of a spirit manifestation was taken, the medium Florence Cook was seated to the right of the room. Cook's spirit form was known as Katie King, and the highly respected scientist and psychic investigator Sir William Crookes took 44 shots of her over three years, after which Katie King disappeared from Cook's séances. The speculation about Florence and her spirit manifestations is rich with juicy gossip and suspicion. She was only 18 in 1874 but Crookes was 42, and was suspected of enjoying a clandestine affair with the teenager. It can be argued Crookes publicly believed in Florence Cook's abilities as a medium only because he dared not compromise his enviable scientific reputation by admitting he was wrong. He was independently wealthy, and one of the most important scientists of the 19th century, in both the fields of physics and chemistry. He had discovered thallium in 1861 and his study of cathode rays laid the ground for atomic physics, so only the most rigid uprightness was attributed to him.

Reports about the Katie King séances are muddled, and there are even inconsistencies in Crookes' reports. Yet he attested to her reality for the rest of his life, saying to The British Association in 1898: 'outside our scientific knowledge there exists a Force exercised by intelligence differing from the ordinary intelligence common to mortals'. But did Crookes actually know that the medium Florence and her spirit Katie were the same person? There were plenty of clues this might have been so. When Sir George Sitwell once seized an apparent spirit manifestation, he found it was Florence herself, in her underwear.

'it was Florence herself, in her underwear'

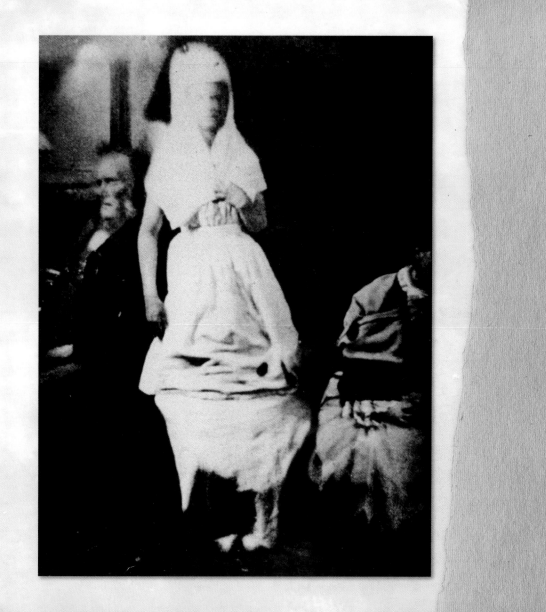

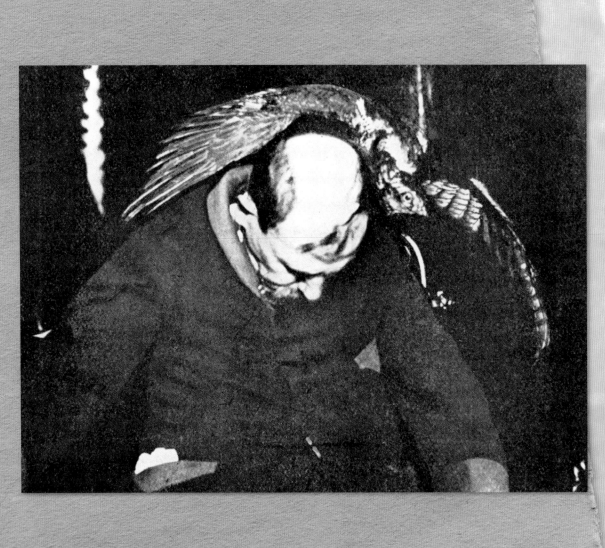

Eagle from the Ectoplasm

LOCATION: Unknown
DATE: 1919

Teofil Modrzejewski had a special claim among the mediums who produced physical phenomena from apparently empty air. He materialized dogs, cats, squirrels, a lion, and, on one auspicious occasion, a primordial man, part human and part ape. Born in Warsaw, Poland, in 1874, he worked as a bank manager and held séances under the pseudonym of Franek Kluski. He came to prominence after 1918 and also differed from other mediums by sometimes performing in a well-lit environment. This photograph was taken at a séance where, 'From the writhing mass of ectoplasm came a whirring and a rustling, then a beating of huge wings. Slowly there emerged a magnificent eagle…' (Barbanell: *The Newsletter*, Noah's Ark Society, September 1994.)

Not surprisingly, there has been considerable controversy concerning the authenticity of this and other phenomena Kluski produced. Consider the bird's size and short beak. These show it's not an eagle but some sort of hawk, something rather easier to conceal and reveal, and Barbanell doesn't explain how the slow cameras of the day managed to take such a sharp picture of the 'beating of huge wings'. The *Journal of the Society for Psychical Research* has featured articles arguing both for and against the authenticity of the photograph, as well as correspondence that continued well into the late 20th century. If the Kluski phenomena were not genuine then at the very least he was a brilliant conjurer and perhaps a mass hypnotist, too. This image retains considerable power and stimulates earnest discussion about the possibility of it being one of very few photographs ever to have been taken of an allegedly materialized bird.

'From the writhing mass of ectoplasm came a whirring and a rustling'

The Ghost of Abraham Lincoln

LOCATION: Studio in New York City, USA
DATE: 1869?

Spirit photographer William H. Mumler didn't know his sitter had lied. She said her name was Mrs. Tundall, and arrived in his studio in a black dress, bonnet and veil. In fact she was Mary Todd Lincoln, the murdered President's widow, something Mumler possibly didn't discover until the photograph he took was developed, clearly showing her dead husband with his hands resting on her shoulders.

'the photograph clearly showed her dead husband with his hands resting on her shoulders'

Mumler is widely credited with discovering spirit photography – inventing it some would say. Originally an amateur photographer who worked engraving jewels in Boston, he was developing self-portraits when he noticed on one plate the extra figure of his cousin, who had died 12 years earlier. He almost immediately became celebrated as a photographer of departed spirits and was so successful he started taking such pictures full time. He then moved to New York, where his work gained much adulation. Other experts tested his methods, but they could not find fraud, and his fame spread to England. His book *Personal Experiences of William H. Mumler in Spirit Photography* is very illuminating about his methods, beliefs, and sitters. Some time around 1872, a young Master Herrod of North Bridgewood, Massachusetts, went into a trance and was photographed with the spirits of Europe, Asia, and America, and there are albums of mothers, fiancées, actresses, and spirit guides all hovering behind the pictures' living subjects. The only thing Mumler didn't see was his downfall, precipitated when it was discovered many of his wraiths were living people. He was acquitted of fraud after a court case, but never recovered and died in poverty in 1884.

The Posing Spirits

LOCATION: Frederick Hudson's studio, London, England
DATE: c.1875

This is attributed to the famous English spirit photographer, Frederick Hudson, whose pioneering studio was at 117 Holloway Road, London. It's said to be an image of his friend Mr. Raby, allegedly with the spirits of The Countess, James Lombard, Tommy, and of Mr. Wootton's mother. Hudson is supposed not to have touched the camera or the film, which was developed by others, as explained in an inscription: 'Obtained by Messrs. Raby, Wootton & Rutherford at Hudson's Studio. At a Séance at Mr. Wootton's the spirits desired him to go to Hudson's promising they would try to produce their likeness. Mr. W. did so, accompanied by his friends. The gentlemen operated themselves without allowing Hudson to take any part in the manipulations.'

> 'could not come up with logical explanations for the abnormal images'

But his friends did nothing to protect the plate from later tampering. Masking and 'Farmer's reducer' could all have been used to remove signs of deception. The editor of the *British Journal of Photography* investigated Hudson's studio the following year (bringing his own plates and chemicals) and could not come up with logical explanations for the abnormal images he also found. If the editor used Hudson's own camera then perhaps there is an explanation. Hudson is alleged to have had a specially adapted Howell camera, which contained a hidden metal frame that could be loaded with transparent waxed paper on to which the required ghostly image could be created. It clicked into place while the plate was exposed, adding its image, and then fell back into its hiding place. But this can't explain how some subjects were given recognizable pictures of dead sons and mothers. Although known to dress up and pose as his own 'ghosts' and to use double exposure for cheating, Hudson was ultimately believed to have leavened his frauds with much genuine spirit photography.

Phantoms in the Basilica

LOCATION: Basilica of Le Bois-Chenu, Domremy, France
DATE: 1925

The powerful provenance of this photograph is vital. It was taken in a much-revered basilica dedicated to St. Joan of Arc. St. Joan's history-changing spiritual experiences, allowing her to recognize an heir to the French throne she had never met and then to lead France to great battle victory, took place in woods close to this basilica. Lady Palmer took the photograph of her friend Miss Townsend and convincingly said no one else was in the basilica. But when the photograph was developed two figures dressed as priests appeared in the image.

'there is scarcely a place more likely in all of France for paranormal happenings'

The age of the photograph and the lack of any other evidence makes judging its veracity a problem. Undoubtedly, both women were aware of the great spiritual associations of the place. The heightened emotion caused by such a mystical setting is often associated with thoughtography. This is where the mind of the subject or the person behind the camera makes images appear spontaneously on film. In the case of this photograph, I think the idea of amateur double exposure can be dismissed as something done consciously. But cameras of the time were hardly reliable and so an involuntary double exposure is always a possibility. Yet there is scarcely a place more likely in all of France for paranormal happenings. What do you think?

The Ghostly Peer in the Library

LOCATION: The library, Combermere Abbey, near Whitchurch, Cheshire, England
DATE: December 5, 1891

The inhabited remains of the 12th-century Benedictine abbey were especially still. Almost everyone was attending the funeral of Lord Combermere, who had been tragically killed in a horse and carriage accident. Miss Sybell Corbet took the opportunity to photograph his lordship's favourite chair in the library and swears neither of the two remaining staff entered that room during the one-hour exposure. She developed the plate herself and then discovered the undersized ghostly image of the dead peer, back in his favourite chair.

> **'and then discovered the undersized ghostly image of the dead peer, back in his favourite chair'**

Sir William Barrett, a leading light in the Society for Psychical Research, originally thought the image was inconclusive, agreeing with others that one of the servants might have forgotten they went into the library. He changed his mind when Lord Combermere's daughter-in-law wrote to say none of the servants resembled the person photographed, and that all his lordship's children were convinced it was him, as reported in the *Journal of the Society for Psychical Research*, December 1895. There remain several problems to resolve if it is to be believed as a genuine ghostly image. For instance, the lord appears not to have any legs and some think his head is not in proportion to the ghostly arm. It is a real mystery but I still feel there could be an alternative non-paranormal explanation. Perhaps there was a lighting anomaly, but more likely a double exposure perpetrated by someone with a sense of humour.

PHOTOGRAPHING THE INVISIBLE

Can we photograph thoughts, the very pictures in our minds? Are there such things as auras, orbs or poltergeists? The notion that thoughts can be transferred directly onto photographic film is generally known as thoughtography. It seems untenable until you look at what Ted Serios produced between 1964 and 1967. The University of Maryland, Baltimore, has a very fine collection of well documented files and photographs produced by Serios which convinced psychic researcher Jule Eisenbud. It seems foolhardy to believe every shot they took was fraudulent, especially because Eisenbud, and other witnesses, often changed the circumstances in which the photographs were taken.

Then, there is the idea that every living thing, including plants, has an aura, and this is something that appears to be demonstrable. Kirlian photography and human aura photography produce images that do what they claim – they record on film that which we do not normally see. The dispute lies in the source of these normally invisible manifestations, and what they can be taken to mean. The fact that bodies emit heat and that all organisms have an effect on their surroundings cannot be denied, but Kirlian photographs take this further, seeming to be able to produce phantom images of parts of, say, a leaf, still attached to the original but actually after it has been physically removed. No special meanings have been attached to such photographs, unlike those of humans. The interpretation of people's health and personality traits from the colour of their auras is very controversial, because they vary so much from exponent to exponent.

The Rosenheim photograph is the only one in this book of alleged poltergeist activity, which is characterized by the moving of furniture and other phenomena caused by an unseen force. More than 40 witnesses swore to what they saw, video recorded the swinging lights you can see, and thorough investigations were done by authorities from the scientific and parapsychology establishment. This event might still be a mystery but no one can say it didn't happen. It's a pity we didn't think to include a DVD with this book...but there's a great idea for the next one.

The photographs that sum up the conunda presented in this chapter the most are those taken by Dr. Baraduc. Immediately after his wife, and then his son, died he took photographs hoping to prove the body has a spirit that survives, but slowly departs. When you look at them every manner of thought possible will go through your mind. What sort of man was he to do such a thing so soon after bereavement? Is it a case of fraud, careless film development, or a technical camera fault? Was there an element of thoughtography, of aura transmission perhaps? Eventually, you will have to ask yourself if you believe in the continuation of the human soul.

A Spirit of Faith

LOCATION: The Holy Heart Hospital, location unknown
DATE: published September 15, 1992

'Father in Heaven – this is a human soul!' That was the reaction of a priest at The Holy Heart Hospital when shown this photograph. An article by Donald Rivers in *Weekly World News* in 1992 also said it showed 'a glowing angelic spirit rising up off the operating table' just as 32-year-old Karin Fischer died and her heart monitor went flat. Peter Valentin, the hospital's director of education, found the image among 72 photographs he took during the operation, and authenticated it. None of the 12 theatre staff saw anything at the time but surgeon Dr. Walter Springer and the biblical scholar Dr. Martin Muller have all been involved in subsequent discussion and research. Pope John Paul II requested a copy of the picture and 'clergymen and scholars throughout Europe' have investigated it.
Well, that is the story.

'a glowing angelic spirit rising up off the operating table'

However, doubts about this well-known photograph arise quickly because the spirit image is so startlingly familiar. The crossed feet make it look suspiciously like a doctored crucifixion image has been added to the original operating theatre photograph by double exposure. Worryingly, despite the apparent provenance often quoted with this photograph, I can find no Holy Heart Hospital that exists and neither Dr. Springer nor Dr. Muller is detectable. But Donald Rivers was a fictional investigative journalist in *The Outer Limits*, a sci-fi television series created in the 1960s, and revived in the 1990s. This is just the sort of paranormal subject he would have relished. Ultimately, I believe each observer will accept the image or reject it based on their personal faith, unless they are a regular reader of *Weekly World News* which published the image. This specialist in spoofs also publishes regular stories of Elvis sightings, of George Bush planning to be the next Pope, and of an affair and marriage between Saddam Hussein and Osama bin Laden.

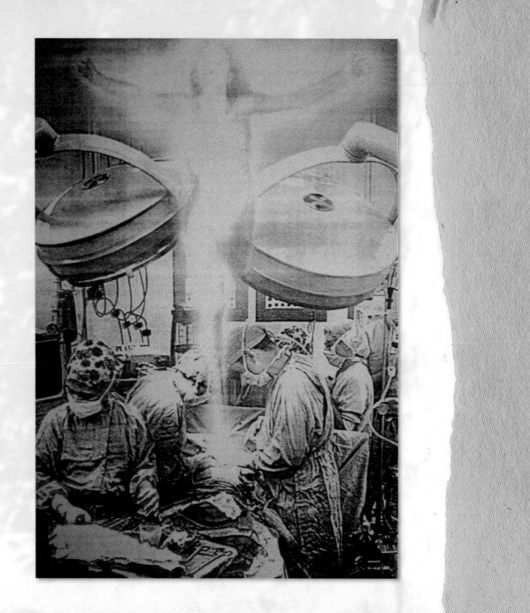

The Releasing of the Soul

LOCATION: Deathbed of Baraduc's wife, France
DATE: 1907

There was a 20-minute gap between these two plates of film capturing an intensely personal deathbed scene. Their similarity is what seems both most chilling and convincing: three clumps of mist hover over the recently dead body. Dr. Baraduc believed he had caught the soul of his wife departing. Hyppolite Baraduc had experimented with spirit photography in late 19th-century France, and also found early examples of what was later coined 'thoughtography'. Someone would concentrate on an image while holding an unexposed photographic plate and an image would appear on it, allegedly psychically. He addressed the French Academy of Medicine on the subject in 1895 and claimed to have invented a 'biometer', which could measure a nervous force and unknown forms of energy outside the human body. His findings about what he called the 'vital force' were published extensively and he wrote a book, *The Human Soul*, in Paris, in 1913.

If you believe that thoughtography is possible then it is likely that Baraduc's elevated emotional state of mind at his time of bereavement could have contributed to the creation of these images. On the other hand, it might have contributed to him making mistakes he did not recollect. But it's the similarity of the soul images that suggests another more mundane explanation. A professional photographer I contacted suggested miniscule pinholes in the bellows behind the lens of an early camera might produce such an effect, especially in an unstable environment on a long exposure. Their uniformity might be because such tiny holes were on one of the bellows' crease lines, the most delicate part of all and very prone to cracking.

'Dr. Baraduc believed he had caught the soul of his wife departing'

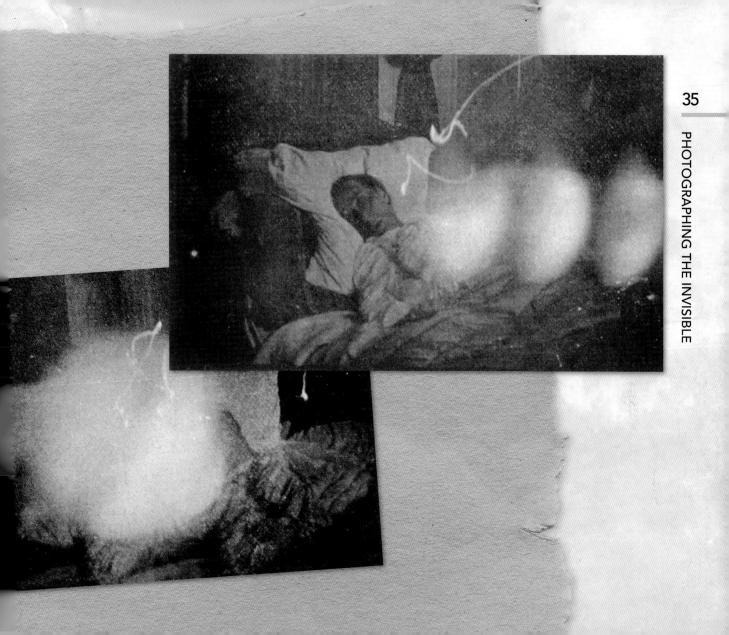

Mystery of the Reattached Leaf Tip

LOCATION: Russia
DATE: 1960s

Do such images prove that all living things produce an aura? These fascinating pictures were produced using a method discovered in Russia in 1939 by scientists Semyon and Valentina Kirlian. Their technique claims to capture the electrical energy currents of living things. To do so, the subject must be in direct contact with the film, 'sandwiched' between two metal plates and then a high-voltage charge is passed through it, which is said to amplify natural biological-energy flows. The effect of this amplification is then recorded directly on to film, giving the sort of results you see opposite. It was also claimed that the technique can recapture the human aura on film, but this is now disputed by the majority of investigators.

In 1966 the Russian researcher Victor Adamenko discovered that by cutting part of a leaf away, and then photographing the original using the Kirlian technique, an outline of the complete shape was still evident, albeit less clearly, as in the smaller green image, left. He continued his exploration and later found a Kirlian image of a human finger, for instance, would change colour according to the stress level of the person concerned. If true, this technique would obviously have medical implications and some practitioners have used it in this way, believing it can demonstrate the effectiveness of acupuncture.

> '**an outline of the complete shape was still evident**'

The sceptical say the effects are possibly caused by moisture in or on the subjects photographed, or by the printing emulsions being displaced during printing. It would also be comparatively simple to produce such images using masking and double-exposure techniques. The image featuring a cross is another example of Kirlian photography, but this time the object is inanimate. The radiation or aura allegedly shows the psychological balance of the wearer of the cross and his or her relationship with it.

In the Highways of the Mind

LOCATION: Probably Denver, Colorado, USA
DATE: 1960s

This clear image of a double-decker bus was allegedly created solely by the projected concentration of Ted Serios' mind energy to make psychic photography or thoughtography. Serios was discovered in 1961, and from 1964 until 1967, Denver psychiatrist, Jule Eisenbud, experimented with him and a Model 95 Polaroid Land camera with black and white film. Serios held the closed camera between his legs, pointed it at his forehead and often used a 'gizmo', a tube of black paper directly on the camera to guide his thoughts more accurately. Many images seemed to be from postcards or books Serios had seen, rather than from pure imagination.

'he did produce plenty of images when many yards from the camera'

Sceptics believed the gizmo allowed Serios to use sleight-of-hand, but he did produce plenty of images when yards from the camera. In fact, this image was produced when Dr. John F. Conger, Dean of the University of Colorado Medical School, held his hand over the gizmo. Sometimes others tripped the camera, at other times Serios was put into a Faraday cage, a metallic enclosure that prevents the entry or escape of an electromagnetic (EM) field, or had to wear clothing provided to avoid objects being concealed. Serios was an alcoholic, he performed best when drunk, exhibited little self-control, and was said to 'wail and bang his head on the floor when things were not going his way'. His talent declined and finally disappeared after 1969. Serios created more than one thousand thoughtographs, and the implacably convinced (but widely debunked) Eisenbud challenged anyone to replicate the same effects, with or without trickery. The challenge was never accepted and noted psychic-sceptic James Randi said, 'If Mr. Serios ... did not use a trick method, all the rules of physics, particularly of optics, everything developed by science over the past several centuries, must be rewritten.'

The Schneider Poltergeist

LOCATION: Königstrasse 13, Rosenheim, Bavaria, Germany
DATE: 1967/8

Whenever 18-year-old Anne-Marie Schneider was around, there were unexplainable noises and frightening phenomena, like these swinging lights captured on videotape. More than 40 people experienced them. In the lawyers' office where she worked, lights exploded unexpectedly and there were countless calls to the talking clock nobody claimed to have made. Then paintings and heavy furniture changed position by themselves. After technicians from Siemens and the Elektrizitätswerk (the German electricity board) couldn't find faults, physicists Dr. Karger of the Max Planck Institute of Plasma Physics and Dr. Zicha from Munich University could only say an unknown form of energy was at work. Then parapsychologist Hans Bender from the Freiburg Institute realized Anne-Marie Schneider seemed to trigger the phenomena and in 1968 made the video recordings.

Poltergeist action, a term covering unexplained noises and the physical moving of furniture, is generally associated with children and young people, especially if they are distressed. Anne-Marie was apparently unhappy at home and disliked her job. The movements ceased when she was eventually married in the 1970s. Nobody seems able to explain if poltergeist or psychokinetic incidents, where things are moved and sounds are made allegedly by the power of someone's mind, are conscious or unconscious. But this is an important picture documenting phenomenon notoriously difficult to photograph. Anne-Marie's baffling case is certainly worthy of further study.

'there were unexplainable noises and frightening phenomena, like these swinging lights'

New Ages of Enlightenment

LOCATION: (far left) Unknown; (near left) Stansted Hall, Stansted, Essex, England
DATE: 1990s

Do we all have an aura, an emanation of rays, which can be used to interpret our mental and physical health? Guy Coggins began photographing auras in the 1970s, using his biofeedback Aura Imager camera. The subject places their hands on metal sensors, which electronically interprets their aura. A polaroid system records their 'colours', but there is no claim actually to photograph the aura. Mediums and others interpret the subject's health, personality, or other matters from the variations of colour produced. When my aura was photographed my face was virtually obliterated by a red aura (near left) whereas others were shades of green, yellow, or blue. My aura was called 'the mask', and said to show I was somewhat sceptical, therefore psychically stopping my energy flow. The far left photograph shows the more customary effect: the woman's upper body is clearly visible, but above her head an explosion of auric energy can also be seen. The clarity of this shot suggests a healthy person of an extrovert nature.

In the digital-image age, most people have forgotten that colours from Polaroid prints change according to the speed of development and can thus be arranged to coincide with predestined outcomes, or be totally random if the developer is inept. There are also many problems with interpreting auras. In some New Age magazines the articles offer a baffling number of contrasting explanations for the same colours. The only consistent links between body, soul and colour are those of the Hindu chakras of the human body, with their seven identified energy centres.

'above her head an explosion of auric energy can also be seen'

The Orbs of Avebury Stone Circle

LOCATION: Avebury, Wiltshire, England
DATE: 1990s

Intriguingly, although often dismissed as an optic effect caused by a digital camera, these floating orbs have been seen by the naked eye. These alleged initial sightings make sceptical explanations ring very hollow indeed. It is true that reports of such floating orbs did increase in the 1990s, at the time digital cameras were being taken up. Other examples were digitally recorded at the nearby Red Lion pub, in 1994.

Sceptics opine the orbs are natural particles, like dust or water droplets, which have been dramatically enhanced by close flashlight and the digital process. Believers counter that the orbs seen with the naked eye have also been recorded on film and on video. The paranormal explanations of the origin of the orbs range from spirit manifestations to precisely the sort of unknown, supernatural energies you expect in such an enchanting place as the Avebury Stone Circle. Well worth a detour.

'precisely the sort of unknown, supernatural energies you expect'

Photographic Phenomena

LOCATION: Chelmsford, Essex, England
DATE: 1960s

Suddenly, happy faces of what must have been spirits were appearing on photographic plates, which were said to have been previously unopened. So were disjointed body parts, and even a building, later found to exist in St. Albans, in Hertfordshire, England. The astonished recipients of these alleged images from the other side were a group of spiritualists who met regularly in the 1960s. The phenomena of images appearing during séances on unused photographic plates and later on film was dubbed 'skotography' (Greek for dark-writing), by Miss Felicia Scatcherd, who died in 1927. Many of the Chelmsford skotographs were acquired by the late Cyril Permutt and donated to the Society for Psychical Research. In an unexplainable coincidence his son now owns a shop on the site of the building in St. Albans.

People are still claiming phenomena of this nature occur. Recent examples were produced in Scole, in Norfolk, England, where a group produced skotographs. In 1982 James Randi, noted psychic investigator, reported he tricked one skotograph artist at a séance into switching marked papers, and found the intended target had already been pre-exposed with a supposed spirit face. And couldn't the skotograph seen here simply be exposed and discarded stock, a photographic plate that had also been degraded by age and the incursion of light or damp? That might explain the inclusion of the St. Albans building in the Chelmsford images.

'The phenomena of images appearing during séances on unused photographic plates was dubbed "skotography"'

What Happened to Tinkerbell?

LOCATION: Penrith, Cumbria, England
DATE: 1994

Do some animals possess senses we human beings have lost, or never had in the first place? This photograph of Tinkerbell apparently in the grip of a curious energy force, while Bunty seems not to care, raises many questions. When the negative and the print were sent to the Society for Psychical Research the question was: 'Do you think it's a trick of the camera or was something paranormal happening?' So far no one has been able to answer. One photographic expert I asked had seen the red-line effect before, but 'never with a distortion as appears with the cat's face…There may be a natural explanation but I don't know of one.'

'there may be a natural explanation but I don't know of one'

The reason for taking the shot is not known and it would be useful to discover what else was going on. For instance, was the child on the sofa taunting or playing with the cats? If the paranormal solution is not accepted, the alternative is rather implausible; an extraordinary coincidence of a lighting or developing problem on the film, exactly where Tinkerbell was tilting her head. Such coincidences must occur, of course, but that doesn't mean we should leave it at that and not also accept the likelihood of an unexplainable paranormal moment having been captured on film. I think it no coincidence cats have been associated with good and bad luck for as long as they have been domesticated. The Egyptians believed them to be sacred, even godlike. We are still not sure how these ancients built the Pyramids, so perhaps there are other mysteries they knew about cats…and about parallel worlds.

LOOKALIKES – BEYOND COINCIDENCE?

A simulacrum is anything that has a superficial likeness to something else. This chapter contains examples that are probably not paranormal but dramatically stretch the bounds of credibility, demanding you make up your mind about what you are observing. Seeing significant shapes while staring

into flames or cloud formations are pastimes we have probably all enjoyed at some stage of our lives. As children we think the Man in the Moon might be real and, if we have been moved by stories of witches in folklore and fairytales, sometimes fear what we think we see in the shapes of trees on dark winter nights. That inner need to make sense of something we don't immediately understand, or which can be interpreted in both good and bad ways, is the basis of the Rorschach inkblot test used by psychology and psychiatry researchers. What subjects say they see in the blots is used to interpret personality traits, using the practicality or bizarreness of their interpretations to help identify their mental state. The outstanding question is whether or not shapes and what they seem to represent can have a paranormal element to them and if they do, are the messages we take helpful and beneficial to the running of our lives?

The alleged sightings of religious figures, most notably of Jesus and the Virgin Mary, have been reported throughout history and it is not therefore surprising to find them appearing in photographs. There were many images of Jesus I could have chosen for the book, and only slightly fewer of the Virgin Mary. An interesting fact I have noticed is that simulacra of the Virgin Mary seem to glow, apparently with a holy light.

An especially charming picture is the one construed as showing the face of a cherub, a baby angel, in the posy of flowers held by a bridesmaid. Paintings we have seen in churches, galleries, and in books have unquestionably conditioned us to have a certain expectation of what a cherub should look like. It could be that presented with a shape it doesn't understand, our brain gives us the most comforting explanation it can, and that in reality they probably do not exist. Even if they do, we don't see them often enough to be able to say, 'This is what a cherub really looks like'. However, to my mind, it's a rather enchanting picture and it always brings a smile when I show it to people. What is astonishing is how detailed the modelling of the face appears to be. And yet it is clearly the folds and shadows of the flowers. A coincidence surely, but what a coincidence. The image certainly has the power to move people, whatever the truth might be. That can't be denied or ignored.

The Belméz faces are an interesting case which perhaps moves beyond the coincidence of a momentary 'trick of the light'. They began to appear in the concrete floor of a small house in Andalucia, in Spain, during 1971. They were photographed extensively and submitted to numerous tests. In the end there was no agreement about how they could have been made fraudulently, and so perhaps they were genuinely paranormal events. Here, your personal belief system takes over. If you admit no possibility of the paranormal then an explanation of fraud or mere coincidence will satisfy you. If you believe unknown forces using energies we still do not understand are possible, then you are justified in accepting them as paranormal.

When you are exploring the paranormal, the simplest or most comforting answer is not always the right answer.

The Madonna of the Fountain

LOCATION: Center Parcs Holiday Village, Norfolk, England
DATE: c.1995

This startling photograph caused a sensation at the time, and no wonder. The outline seen in the fountain could hardly be anything other than a Madonna and Child. The outline of the cloak seems unmistakable and so does its unworldly radiance. And look at the swaddled baby in her arms. He seems to be transparent, supernatural, just as you'd expect of the Christ-child.

> '**the cloak seems unmistakable and so does its unworldly radiance**'

Moving water is often associated with the apparent appearance of spirits, especially those associated with religion. Its imagery of purification, its sparkling clarity, and swirling movements are positive and life-affirming factors making something we think we see much more acceptable than, say, a possible ghost in a cemetery. So yes, this might be one of the rare pictures taken of a Marian appearance. But there are times when our brain translates something it does not understand into something familiar, even if it is actually fooling both itself and you. It's a way of reducing fear, tension, and unfounded suspicion. A way of bringing order to chaos.

A Cherub Posing in a Wedding Posy?

LOCATION: Unknown
DATE: 1960s

It's a picture I always show without prior comment when giving talks on anomalous or unusual photographs. Not everyone spots it straight away, but hundreds of people have immediately seen the face gazing out from the top of the girl's wedding posy as a charming cherub. Cyril Permutt, an important 20th-century psychic researcher, was sent this photograph in 1980 by the girl's aunt who felt some concern about it. Mr. Permutt replied encouragingly, saying he believed the image was not harmful in any way, adding, 'this photograph shows signs of psychic or paranormal influence.' Certainly no one I have shown it to has felt it harbours anything unpleasantly psychic or 'harmful'. It seems more often to be regarded as something holy, no doubt because this is generally the quality attributed to cherubs and other angels. This makes the bridesmaid a refreshing antidote to some of the more sinister images in this book. If you'd like to see more alleged images of angels I recommend the website *angelsghosts.com*.

I can't say for certain that a tiny angelic creature has hidden in the flowers on this happy day and then artlessly popped out for a look just as the shot was taken. I've included it because it's a very good example of a simulacrum or superficial likeness that is hard to explain in normal ways. And because it makes so many people feel good.

'this photograph shows signs of psychic or paranormal influence'

The Virgin in the Trees

LOCATION: Near Metz, Alsace, France
DATE: Unknown

There is definitely a startling draped figure here that looks like the Virgin Mary, high in the tree on the left of the church. This image has never been claimed to be the physical presence of the Mother of Christ but something visionary, inspirational rather than devotional. The image is a particular rarity because although thought to appear often, Marian visions are rarely photographed (I have included one other on page 89, captured in Karácsond, Hungary). Other appearances, without photographs, have famously included Medjugorje, in Croatia, and Lourdes, in France, both of which have a vast literature documenting the appearances. Less well known is the appearance of her image in a tree in Watsonville, California, reported in the *Fortean Times* in 1997.

The Roman Catholic faith is usually very sceptical about these sightings and Popes have been hesitant to grant paranormal or saintly status unless the evidence is absolutely conclusive. The stereotypical iconography of the modestly veiled Virgin Mary with Jesus in her arms is commonly spotted in caves and other rock formations, even in water, as seen on page 53. These can be simply explained by her image being more easily recognizable than, say, Joseph. Yet, looking again, the image could be of him or any other biblical character. When you look closely to see how the wall of the church and the trunk of the tree define the shape, you are compelled to interpret the picture as a coincidence of viewpoint. But is it not remarkable how perfectly it holds together, with the branches tracing the drapery of the Virgin's robes?

'Marian visions are rarely photographed'

Indelible Faces in the Floor

LOCATION: Bélmez de la Moraleda, Andalucia, Spain
DATE: August 23, 1971

These pictures are certainly inexplicable and I defy anyone not to be mystified or moved. In fact they have been dubbed 'the most important paranormal phenomenon' of the 20th century. In 1971 a remarkable discovery was made by Doña Maria Gómez Pereira. On the concrete floor of the kitchen in her small house in the Andalucian village of Bélmez there was a face gazing up at her. It appeared to be painted, yet was resistant to scratching. Her son Miguel broke up the flooring because they found it disturbing and then new concrete was laid. Within a week the same image had returned. This attracted so much publicity the mayor ordered it to be cut out and kept behind glass and soon hundreds were visiting the house to see it and others, which slowly appeared. Meanwhile excavation discovered human bones and the haunting realization that most of the street was built over a graveyard. During the following months other faces appeared and a total figure of 18 was declared at one point. None of the faces were susceptible to any cleaning agent and couldn't be scratched. When some were covered with a transparent film for protection they continued to change, seen as proof of paranormal origins.

'excavation discovered human bones and the haunting realization that most of the street was built over a graveyard'

The Bélmez Faces have been very extensively researched and tested. Although signs of brush marks were detected, opinions differed on the presence of paint. The general view is the images were created by using chemicals which bonded atomically with the structure of the concrete and were light sensitive, like the silver nitrate used in traditional photography, thus explaining the slow appearance and fading. Yet even though there seems to be scientific consensus about fakery, no one has come up with a convincing, universally acceptable explanation for the faces of Bélmez. Perhaps there isn't one?

Christ in the Alpine Snow

LOCATION: Swiss Alps
DATE: 1958

The photographer of this picture was an atheist until he had a sudden strange compulsion to take a shot through the window of the plane in which he was travelling. What he captured made him a believer immediately. This stylized portrait of Christ, seemingly formed by snow and rocks, is certainly a startling simulacrum, and its mystic quality cannot be immediately dismissed or quickly forgotten. Neither has it been. It was first published in 1958, was repeated in 1965, and then used as 'the most famous picture we have ever printed' in the *Sunday People*'s five-thousandth issue in 1977.

'What he captured made him a believer immediately'

The popular press enjoys publishing such controversial pictures, making no profound claim for them and taking no responsibility for their veracity. They attract attention and so sell papers and magazines, and the media says it is ultimately the public's choice whether they believe the images are what they appear to be. As with most of the images in this chapter, the circumstances of the picture do not particularly encourage the belief that there is some sort of supernatural presence or apparition. It is surely a coincidence – a trick of the light. Nevertheless, one can hardly help marvelling at such a coincidence.

Sacred Elephant in the Sky

LOCATION: Chiang Mai, Northern Thailand
DATE: 1994

David Shurville didn't recognize the white, elephant-shaped cloud until his film had been developed. But there it is, exactly where anyone interested in Buddhism and the paranormal would want it to be, ideally positioned over the golden chedi, or spire, of an important temple's pagoda, which is supported by more massive carved elephants. It could hardly be thought more sacred or more propitious. This is because before Buddha was born his mother is alleged to have dreamed of a white elephant and so they are closely associated with great events and good luck. Thus the very rare birth of a white elephant is treated as especially auspicious, and in Thailand such animals always become the property of the monarch.

Of course, looking for shapes in clouds is something we have all enjoyed, and so have people throughout history. For instance, a painting by Piero Della Francesca of 1460 from his *Légende de la Croix* series shows a cloud formation that has been interpreted as showing flying saucers. The *Fortean Times* regularly prints pictures of clouds readers have interpreted to their advantage or disadvantage. What you think depends on what you believe about there being another world, which can sometimes break through the separating veils to warn or encourage us. It's very comforting to think so, and there's just as much evidence for as there is against.

'It could hardly be thought more sacred or more propitious'

The Tumbling Ghost of Lavardin

LOCATION: Church in Lavardin, near Vendôme, France
DATE: September, 1990

The moving but shapeless phantasm is curious and convincing enough, but turn the page upside down and it's much more clearly human, angelic even, perhaps caught in the middle of a joyous paranormal tumble. The photographer, a Mr. Culley, confirmed the apparition was only on one of a number of pictures he took at the same time. The shot was sent to Dr. Vernon Harrison, an ex-president of the Royal Photographic Society and expert on anomalous photographs. He wrote:

'The "clouds" here are wholly confined to the picture frame and are not due to leakage of light into the film cassette. In all the other pictures the behaviour of film and camera is quite normal. The structure of the "cloud" does not suggest it results from internal reflections of bright light within the lens or camera body … Uneven development would not affect just one frame leaving all the others perfect.'

'it is hard to find a rational explanation for the anomaly'

In fact, it's agreed all round that it is hard to find a rational explanation for the anomaly. It is tempting to think that it might be somehow caused by light streaming in from the upper window, and in 2007 it was suggested to me it could simply be a tissue or something similar wafting though the air that was caught on this picture and is thus another case of photographer blindness. Actually, calling the image the Tumbling or Upside-Down Ghost can be very unhelpful when searching for a truth about something puzzling. Expectations have already been aroused by the nature of the subject and the easy pleasure of finding what one is looking for is something encouraged by both our conscious and unconscious minds. But if a clever name stops us looking harder or thinking further the real mystery might be obfuscated, lost to us forever.

The Mystery of Brixton's Shroud Image

LOCATION: Mostyn Road Methodist Church, Brixton, London, England
DATE: First noticed in 1948

Whatever your faith or belief system there's little doubt that the image of the man's face on the wall is startlingly similar to that on the famous Turin Shroud, the cloth supposedly wound around Christ's body after he was taken from the Cross. The photograph was sent to the Society for Psychical Research only in 1995 with a very brief covering note that frustratingly left many questions unanswered. However, the letter approached the subject with a very common-sense attitude, neither implying nor inferring anything. We can probably conclude from this at least that the photographer does not seem to have been motivated by his own beliefs and was simply recording what he saw.

In 1948 when this shot was most likely taken, the magnificently spired Mostyn Road Methodist Church was awaiting restoration after it had been very badly damaged during the Second World War. The area of wall or ceiling appears to have survived undamaged and is above a curtained area which may have been an altar. It's not known what the markings are; they could be bomb damage or simply damp or mould.

> '**startlingly similar to that on the famous Turin Shroud**'

Often a suggested interpretation tells us more about the character of the photographer or the reporter than the actual image itself. One person sees the face of Christ or God, perhaps also believing in some direct personal contact, whilst another sees a damp patch on the wall. If a believer in the Christian faith wishes to accept this was indeed a sign of some holy presence, then who am I to contradict it in the absence of other evidence?

An Angel in the Basement

LOCATION: Unknown
DATE: 1990s?

There's no hard and fast rule about where you see angels, spirits, or ghosts, although a basement is a somewhat unexpected place to see angels. Yet this is how the photograph was described when I found it on a website devoted to alleged appearances by angels. The lack of any hard evidence for such a photograph makes it impossible to come to any firm conclusions. The internet has allowed a host of interesting images to come to light, many of which seem on the face of it to be genuine mysteries, but so often without even a date or location, one has to be wary of making any great claim for them. The figure is boxed in the lower right-hand side of the print. You'll find what looks very much like a halo around the head, and this possibly contributed to the identification; a white collar reinforces the notion this is perhaps a nun, something quite holy. I'm just as fascinated by the mist appearing at the upper right-hand side of the print, which could also do with some clarification.

The sceptic would probably suggest a practical explanation here, saying that there is no such thing as an angel in this picture, but that the brain translates a combination of light and shade into something recognizably human. The function is called pareidolia, possibly stemming from the evolutionary need to recognize and interact with other human faces, most importantly our parents in infancy. It's just as likely a lighting anomaly or some glitch in the chemicals used in the film's development produced the strange effect. But plausible scientific explanations might be just another way of calming us, so we don't have to grapple with paranormal possibilities. You have to make up your own mind.

'a white collar reinforces the notion this is perhaps a nun'

Disembodied Faces in the Waves

LOCATION: from SS *Watertown*, Pacific Ocean
DATE: December 1924

James Courtney and Michael Meehan were buried at sea on December 4, 1924 while they were working on board the U.S. tanker SS *Watertown*, after gas fumes suffocated them. It is said images of the men first appeared on the side of the ship from which they had been committed. Then it is alleged several crew members saw their disembodied ghostly heads in the waves, about forty feet away and for up to ten seconds at a time. On a return journey through the same waters, the ship's captain, Keith Tracey, took a set of six photographs. When shipping company employee James Patton had the film developed in New York, one of the shots showed the faces of the two men in the sea. The camera and film were investigated by the Burns Detective Agency and found to be genuine, and psychical researcher, Hereward Carrington, could only suggest the faces might have been 'thought-forms' or thought photographs, created by strong images of the dead men in the onlookers' minds.

Unfortunately the original photograph cannot be found, making much scrutiny of the image purely speculative. One of my problems is how similar the two faces appear, both wearing moustaches and both with very sunken, black eyes, but perhaps that's how many men looked at the time. The out-of-focus problem means waves or rocks may have produced this illusion, but this can't be checked because no one knows now if these images appeared close to a coast or well out at sea. Anyway, each of the reports of the sightings is quite different, making the photograph an eternal mystery.

'ghostly heads in the waves, about forty feet away'

EVERYDAY ANOMALIES

Most of the pictures in this chapter, and most of the best examples of 'ghost' photographs, were not taken by investigators staking out haunted locations in the hope of capturing something strange on camera. They were taken by ordinary people and intended to be of ordinary things – simple snaps of friends and family. But then, and often after having forgotten about them for some time, they noticed something strange, something anomalous on the image that should not, surely could not, be there. In many cases they sent their pictures to organizations like the Society for Psychical Research and the photographs and the stories that came with them were subjected to close scrutiny. Often this provided a simple explanation. But not always.

Many of our selection here have not appeared in print before. None of them seems to have an obviously fraudulent origin and I have sought as much detail as possible about the places and circumstances. On the technical side I sought the help of professional photographers who alerted me to many possible explanations of strange appearances in photographs. These include camera shake or subject movement creating blurring; lighting flare and light trails forming fogs or shafts of light; hair on or near the lens; dust or pollen in the air; imperfections in film or during the development process; and even the effect of smoke or breath. I learned to be especially wary of 'camera-strap syndrome', where a part of the strap falls unnoticed over the lens and, because it is so close, leaves a blurry and indistinct smudge on the photograph. That's amazingly common. Once you add deliberate fraud to that list, mistaken identity and defective memory, it seems a wonder any photograph ever manages to remain unexplained or anomalous. But some do.

Supposing you are presented with something anomalous, potentially paranormal, I would urge you to try to photograph it if possible.

simple advice to avoid the above mentioned pitfalls would be to make sure that you hold the camera very still – hold your breath when you press the shutter – avoid using flash and check that no stray hair, cigarette smoke, or the camera trap is compromising the shot. Maurice Townsend also advises that if you are using a Polaroid or digital camera, which shows results at once, then take several frames. This will either confirm the presence of the anomaly, something for which any investigator will be exceptionally grateful, or show it to be a one-shot mystery.

For serious photographers on location and with the time to prepare, it's a good idea to have a 'witness' camera. Simon Earwicker suggests using two cameras synchronized together with a cable release. One should have a flash and one without, and ideally one should have a wide-angle lens. This way the simultaneous images will immediately reveal whether a technical problem is the cause of the anomaly. And if two pictures show the anomaly from a different angle it eliminates the possibility that it is a trick of the light dependent on viewpoint.

As you read this chapter I would particularly encourage you to use the investigative guidelines given in the introduction. And then you might want to explore your own photograph albums and boxes, your discs and videos to see if you possess any anomalous shots of your own.

Black Abbot in a Haunted Graveyard

LOCATION: St. Mary's churchyard, Prestbury, Gloucestershire, England
DATE: November 22, 1990

The village of Prestbury, near Cheltenham, in Gloucestershire, is a popular location for alleged sightings of ghosts and other paranormal activity. As early as 1981 it was being referred to as 'The Most Haunted Village' in competition with the other famously haunted village of Pluckley, in Kent, and a current BBC website draws attention to its various paranormal phenomena. This spooky image was captured when, Derek Stafford, a photographer, was taking shots of the floodlit gravestones in St. Mary's churchyard. He was sure that no-one else was present in the graveyard as he did this, but on subsequent development the film image of a black hooded figure (the ghostly abbot?) appeared on the last slide.

According to Richard Jones (in *Haunted Britain and Ireland,* 2001) the Black Abbot, 'appears most often at Christmas, Easter and All Souls Day.' The ghost evidently passes through the graveyard before disappearing through the wall of Reform Cottage in the High Street, whereupon poltergeist activity is heard emanating from the attic. Further stories tell of knocks being heard on the door and of a passage that links the 16th-century cottage with the nearby church – possibly used as an escape route for the monks in difficult times. The garden may have been used as a burial ground when the church owned the surrounding property. It is not known why the abbot would be haunting this area unless he still feels that he is attached to the property in some timeless link

> 'the ghost passes through the graveyard before disappearing through the wall of Reform Cottage'

A Ghostly Arm-pull in Manila

LOCATION: Manila, Philippines
DATE: 2000s

Is this ghostly figure trying to get in the picture? Does the spirit have some connection with the girls? The correct scale of the figure and the exact placement of their hand on the girl's arm seems to make an accidental double exposure unlikely. These Filipino good friends were strolling in a newly developed part of Manila and decided they wanted a shot to record their time together. One of them asked a total stranger to take a picture, using the camera of a Nokia 7250 phone. The astonishing result shows a phantasmic figure pulling at the arm of the girl on the right. The shot was aquired via The Ghost Research Society and they report that neither of the girls was aware of anything strange happening at the time, and that it 'seems to be quite a friendly spirit'. The hold on the arm appears to be quite firm, not a gentle touch, so if it were somehow a real person you would expect her to be reacting. Some say the phantom arm-puller looks like a woman, others that it's a man, but the lack of malevolence is generally agreed upon.

It's hard to be certain in this digital age, but it's considered unlikely you could make a double-exposure on the camera of a phone. Yet with a digital image, it would be the easiest thing in the world for a computer whiz to have doctored the original shot. The answer of course would be to interview the girls. But who are they? Do you know them? Are you one of them? We are waiting for your call.

'a phantasmic figure pulling at the arm of the girl on the right'

Birthday Intruders

LOCATION: Bromsgrove, Worcestershire, England
DATE: February 23, 1993

Look who has also come to the party uninvited. Phillip Fowler has taken a flash photograph of son Matthew waiting to blow out his birthday candles, and disembodied faces seem to be floating out of the cake, but are corpselike and certainly not interested in what's about to happen. Mr. Fowler sent this photograph to the Society for Psychical Research seeking no publicity for the shot, but simply asking for clarification of the birthday-party intruders. He used a Hanimex focus-free 35mm self-winding camera with flash and with the lights off to enhance the candles on the cake. He took a picture directly before this one with the lights on, but it included no unusual extra figures. The negatives were examined and the company processing the images could not explain how the faces appeared and claimed no tampering had taken place. Another photographic expert thought the extra image to be a reflection from a television set. None of the Fowlers' friends or family could identify the mysterious 'intruders' and Matthew says he did not experience anything strange at the time.

'disembodied faces seem to be floating out of the cake, corpselike'

In my experience, people are often unsettled by this image. If the circumstances in which it was produced are true, this photograph certainly appears to show something very strange indeed, truly anomalous. Every one of the neutral observers I've shown it to, people who neither believe in the paranormal nor hold anything against the possibility of unknown phenomena existing, has been intrigued and, sometimes, disturbed. It would help if someone could identify the biggest head. Can you?

A Baffling Presence on Calvary Hill

LOCATION: Church of the Holy Sepulchre, Jerusalem, Israel
DATE: c. 1990

Visiting the Church of the Holy Sepulchre is always a spiritual experience. It's built over the site of Calvary Hill, where Christians believe Jesus Christ was crucified. But would you expect to capture what looks like a real spirit on film? The in-laws of Mrs. Thompson of Dunstable, Bedfordshire, England, thought nothing of their snap, but Mrs. Thompson thought it showed a ghostly nun. Maurice Grosse, the Chairman of the Spontaneous Cases Committee for the Society for Psychical Research, replied to her saying:

> 'The cloud effect could be construed as the result of a double exposure due to a fault with the camera ... However, the configuration ... does not seem to justify this conclusion ... The base of the 'cloud' clearly shows two shoes, complete with laces, and what could be construed as a hand or foot stretching forward ... there appears to be a shadow on the lower part of the left hand [sic] shoe ... This cloud type effect is not unknown ... in places of religious significance, but it is most unusual to see such detail ... it is certainly one of the strangest configurations I have seen ...'

'certainly one of the strangest configurations I have seen'

I first thought a cat had walked through the shot. But closer scrutiny showed other light effects above the main image and the foot and shoe mentioned. There is also the chance of this being some curious play of light in dust in the air. But are those modern shoes, and why is it common for pictures like this to be 'not unknown ... in places of religious significance?' Calvary Hill has more than one anomaly to give up.

Who is the Lady in Blue?

LOCATION: Woodcroft, Boar's Hill, Oxford, England
DATE: May 20, 1990

Does the second of these two photographs, taken moments apart, also include the young man's dead grandmother? His mother, Mrs. Seligman, believes the apparition is her late mother-in-law, wearing the low-heeled, dark shoes and blue or blue-grey skirt and woollen top she wore when she was alive. Photography expert Dr. Vernon Harrison, an ex-President of the Royal Photographic Society, had this to say:

> 'I can think of no normal explanation … The 'skirt-like' object is in a dark blue colour not found elsewhere in the picture and it is opaque … Below the 'skirt' emerges what appears to be a bare human right foot, the toes of which are clearly visible … could be interpreted as the figure of a child or diminutive woman, bare-footed and wearing a dark blue skirt extending almost to the ankles and a bluish-grey shawl … I do not think that any of the usual explanations (e.g. double exposure, stray light, misinterpretation of patterns, etc.) can apply here.'

I find it hard to dismiss such an opinion from Dr. Harrison. But if there are no technical problems with the photographs, and their backgrounds are identical except for the figure in the blue shawl, what other explanation is there? You know the answer.

'I do not think that any of the usual explanations can apply here'

The Little Girls

LOCATION: Near Beck Hole, North Yorkshire Moors, England
DATE: 11 August 1982

This was intended to be a picture of a little girl playing by a stream, but turned out to be something much more mysterious. After development, and clearly shown on the negative, was what appeared to be another girl or girls in Victorian or Edwardian dress in the background. The father of the small girl shown in the foreground took this photograph between 2pm and 3pm on a hot sunny afternoon when no one else was in view. It is not known who or what it is, but the photographer is certain the anomaly was not there when he took the shot. Professional photographer and psychic investigator Cyril Permutt was sufficiently intrigued to show this photograph to a medium who provided a reading from it. Apparently the medium could 'see' various figures in addition to the white form and was able to give specific dates. It was not reported whether the family of the girl found these to be significant.

'It is not known who or what it is, but the photographer is certain the anomaly was not there when he took the shot'

The idea that the anomalous figures are in historic dress appeals to the notion that the sighting of a ghost may be some sort of 'time slip': the ghost getting on with its own business in its own time but somehow momentarily visible to another time, a century later. This provides an interesting and logical explanation for the sightings of monks and nuns walking through ancient cloisters and other such traditional ghost stories.

Teacher Spectre in the Playground

LOCATION: Playground, somewhere in England
DATE: June 1977

These excited schoolchildren thought they were simply posing for a souvenir of their Silver Jubilee outing. What they didn't expect is people would be still looking at their photograph 30 years later. That's because a fleeting figure can clearly be seen behind the group moving from right to left, dressed in what appears to be a grey, full-skirted dress with a big white collar, and with her brown hair tied back in a bun. The baffling photograph was one of several taken at the time on an Ilford Sportsman camera. Mrs. Gregory, the photographer, was convinced there was no one behind the group and the shot taken immediately before (not shown here) seems to prove that. So what can the explanation be?

'a fleeting figure can clearly be seen behind the group'

A photographic expert felt it was unlikely to be camera shake or a sticky shutter, because much more of the picture would be blurred. It's obviously a dull day and the shutter speed must have been quite slow but the children are all more or less in focus. This is a case where photographer's blindness must be suspected, that is, another person did indeed walk hurriedly behind the children but was not noticed through the lens. Yet look again. Doesn't the figure seem to be in rather old-fashioned clothes, the sort you'd expect a teacher from former times to wear? The possibilities of fraud or accident are both ways to resolve the problem, and so is a paranormal solution. Perhaps this really is a privileged glimpse of a departed but still unsettled teacher, doomed forever to anxiously patrol the children in her playground?

The Miraculous Madonna of Karácsond

LOCATION: Karácsond Church, near Budapest, Hungary
DATE: September 1989

This puzzling photograph is on display in the church where it was taken, a clear indication that priest Béla Kovács, and his congregation, believe a genuine miracle occurred here. They accept unquestioningly, as do many others, that it shows the Virgin Mary. Some see her holding the infant Jesus. Others think he stands in front of her. Contradictory claims say the image was captured either by a taxi driver or by the art restorer Károly Ligeti, who also says he actually saw this vision, not noticed by other people in the church, while standing on some scaffolding. The incumbent priest asserted there was no similar statue in the church that might have been catching the sun and thus creating a reflection that could be interpreted as such a vision.

Various organizations have studied the photograph, including the Hungarian Press Agency and Britain's Independent UFO Network and claim there had been no tampering. Unsurprisingly there are differing opinions, as you can see for yourself in issues of the *Fortean Times* in 1994 and 1996. These range from accusations of outright deception by Ligeti to a lighting or development gremlin. Those convinced of paranormal origins say genuine religious feelings allowed him to project a form of mind energy so powerful it could also be photographed. Janet Bord, the researcher of Fortean phenomena, wrote in the *Fortean Times* that an outright pronouncement of faking would be 'somewhat ill-judged and hasty'.

'a form of mind energy so powerful it could also be photographed'

Hooded Figure of Les Caves Huguenots

LOCATION: Huguenot Caves, Ardèche Region, France
DATE: October 1986

The glaring ethereal light could be just about anything, but the hand that emerges from it makes you wonder. The caves of the southwestern regions were once the main hiding places in France for Huguenots, Protestant worshippers who were banned by Louis IX. Their history of persecution is bloody and tragic. To anybody in the least sensitive, these caves positively reek of their turbulent history. Mrs. Keighly wanted only to photograph the ceiling stalactites and had asked to be left alone for a few moments in the lower cave to achieve a clear view. She felt and saw no one beside her. She took her pictures with a 'cheap Kodak disc camera' and these were developed by a photographer in Milford-on-Sea, Lymington, England. When she noticed the anomaly shown here, she sent the photograph to the Society for Psychical Research. Dr. Harrison researched the photograph and found it to be 'very curious'. He felt the 'hooded figure' could be 'the back view of a robed figure, wearing head dress Arab fashion', but that it could also be 'the effect of stray light'. However, several fingers appear to be emerging from the robes and resting on the safety rail, which he found baffling if this were simply a lighting manifestation. Dr. Harrison's conclusion was that the photograph should be consigned to the 'unexplained' file, as a definite anomaly.

Another photographic expert believes there must have been an object in the foreground Mrs. Keighly had inadvertently photographed, perhaps something also held in her hands and which had slipped into frame while she was concentrating on the roof formations, and then bleached out by the closeness of the flashlight. That's an easy explanation, but considering the history of the caves, could you be sure it was the right one? And why should it be Arabic headdress? Might not this just as plausibly be the back of a radiant Madonna figure?

> 'To anybody in the least sensitive, these caves positively reek of their turbulent history'

The Puzzle of the Painted Monk

LOCATION: Haworth Moor, Yorkshire, England
DATE: February 2004

Is this a real place almost too picturesque to be true, and with a real ghost? Or is it a manipulated image that only owns up to its fraudulence when blown up? A Mrs. Friar sent the digital photograph to the Society for Psychical Research, saying:

> '... she [Mrs. Friar's niece] took several shots of Haworth Moor landscape for her current Art project and was curious, on downloading the following images, to see another figure which had certainly not been there when taking the picture ... to me it is the "archetypal grey-hooded figure roaming the moors" (the figure appears quite ethereal compared to the man in black behind it on the path) ...'

'the figure appears quite ethereal compared to the man in black'

Mrs. Friar and her art-student niece found the picture to be 'rather fanciful, but quite intriguing nevertheless'. Indeed. There are definitely some unexplained or unexplainable details open to many interpretations. There is a jagged black diagonal line behind the hooded figure and the 'real' man in black has a forked-lightning effect apparently ending in his hands, plus a curious brown shape behind him. These look like marks or tears consistent with an old print rather than a digital image. The most obvious possibility is the art student deviously manipulated the digital image as part of her course work, but didn't tell her aunt. Look at the close-up of the supposed monk and it looks very much as though he has been quickly, impressionistically painted in, as do the bracken and grasses. Of course the student simply might not have noticed someone else all wrapped up for a chilly February walk. Or, just possibly, she might have photographed the ghost of a lonely monk walking on the moors.

Who's That in the Pilot's Seat?

LOCATION: Fleet Air Arm Station, Yelverton, Somerset, England
DATE: August 1987

Mrs. Sayer was adamant that she was definitely the only person sitting in the helicopter when this shot was taken, without flash. At the time she also remarked on how cold it felt, even though it was very hot that day. Unusually, there is also powerful added proof that something odd was taking place. That same day, Mrs. Sayer told Maurice Grosse of the Society for Psychical Research: 'The husband of the friend with us also took a photograph of his wife a few minutes after my one, without a flash, but when his roll of film was developed, this photograph of me was the only one on the roll, which was otherwise blank.' The helicopter was on display as part of an exhibition of aircraft used in the Falklands War. Military security meant information about the helicopter's use in the Falklands could not be obtained, so it's not possible to say if someone died in it and is haunting it, but that is the most obvious paranormal explanation.

This is a very interesting photograph, which came to light in 1995 and for which I can offer no logical explanation. I've spent a considerable amount of time with an expert photographer discussing the image and he offered no enlightenment except for discounting a lighting effect or chemical spillage. Thus we seem to be left with two possible conclusions. Either Mrs. Sayer and her friends for some reason produced a fraudulent picture, then waited seven years to reveal it, or a very strange anomalous phenomenon has been captured, quite possibly a ghost. Or is this another example of our mind jumping to a conclusion that is not wholly supported by what our eyes can see?

'powerful added proof that something odd was taking place'

The Sleeping Ghost

LOCATION: Rossal House, Sunbury-on-Thames, Surrey, England
DATE: Unknown

There seems to be one blindingly obvious question here. Why would anyone looking for ghosts under test conditions take a photograph of a chair? Actually, there is a second one. Why would a ghost wrap itself in a blanket? This image is supposed to have been caught by inventor and electro-metallurgist Sherard Cowper-Coles during experiments with Admiral Moore, a member of the Ghost Club. It was taken in daylight in the sitting room where a vacant armchair, covered in pink and white striped chintz, stood by the window. There was no one else in the sitting room and the transparent figure has never been identified. It should be added that Cowper-Coles' wife, also a scientist, attested she had actually seen the ghost thought to haunt Rossal.

'she had actually seen the ghost thought to haunt Rossal'

The face itself is fascinating. The painted eyebrows and curly blonde hair look very much like the challenging fashions adopted by the young women of the 1920s and 30s, and Cowper-Coles died in 1936. Or do you think it more like a Georgian gentleman, bewigged and powdered? The photographers certainly thought it a man. Either way, the photograph has all the hallmarks of a simple double exposure, but would such worthy gentlemen be indulging in fraud, or unaware if a photographic mishap had occurred under their so-called test conditions? Anyway, wouldn't the gents or their friends have recognized the face if a living person were indeed involved? You have to ask, just who is the wrapped-up person resting their head so wearily on Cowper-Coles' chair? When did he or she live?

The Ghost of Hanging Tree

LOCATION: Cromdale Church, Morayshire, Scotland
DATE: October 9, 1976

Do you know what a real ghost looks like? It's not often they're like the vaporous, indistinct shapes depicted by Hollywood. In fact, most of the cases investigated by the Society for Psychical Research during the past 125 years have looked like you and me, just as they were when they were supposedly alive. So what's that in this photograph of an old tree at Cromdale Church, known as the 'hanging tree', captured by a Mrs. Ramsay? The reputation of the tree, formerly used as a gallows, is linked to the tale of a battle that took place here between the Grants and the Jacobites, and one of the tombstones does mark the grave of a member of the Grant family.

'Being hanged publicly would make a good case for this wraith being created by the terror of the victim'

There is a widely held belief that if there was extreme emotion at the time of someone's death, this will continue to stimulate inexplicable events for many years into the future. Being hanged publicly from a tree would make a good case for this wraith in Mrs. Ramsay's shot having been created by the terror of the victim. The great problem here is the lack of focus. It means this is just as likely to be a simulacrum, something unknown, but so like something we know that the brain explains it in terms we readily accept – rightly or wrongly. So, the blurry spectre could just be a trick of the light, but it certainly looks like a hanged corpse with a hooded head, as long as you believe this is what a ghost looks like.

The Watcher of St. Botolph's Balcony

LOCATION: St. Botolph's Church, Bishopsgate, London, England
DATE: May 15, 1982

Mr. and Mrs. Brackley had got themselves to the church well on time. He had come to photograph a wedding but, because they were early, secured permission to photograph the church's interior. He used a ten-second exposure on a tripod-mounted camera because of the lack of sufficient lighting. They were both adamant there was no one else in the church at the time and that there is no evidence that their equipment nor the development of the film was faulty. But they had been watched by a strange robed figure on the balcony in the top right of the picture.

'they had been watched by a strange robed figure'

St. Botolph's Church has a tragic history, as have many churches in London, with many unnamed plague victims of 1665 hurriedly buried unmarked in its graveyard. Because the spectral figure appears to be robed, and a wedding was about to take place, it's possible a member of the church's hierarchy or one of the choir did walk in briefly, notice the photographer and turn around, hoping not to have been spotted. How would someone up there know where the camera was pointed? If the picture is consciously fraudulent then a professional photographer like Brackley has the best chance of getting away with it. But listen to what is supposed to have happened some years later. A builder contacted Mr. Brackley, saying while he was working in St. Botolph's crypt he had accidentally disturbed some coffins, one of which was opened to reveal a body with a similar face to the one in his picture. This sensational message seems impossible, for surely a face in a coffin would be considerably deteriorated?

Unknown Hand in the Veil

LOCATION: St. Austin's Roman Catholic Church, Merseyside, Liverpool, England
DATE: June 25, 1994

Did Melanie Roberts' deceased father give his daughter a helping hand of support on the day she was welcomed into the Catholic Church? Look at the veil on her left side and you will see what looks like a hand wearing a ring. Mrs. Jean Roberts, Melanie's mother, sent this photograph to the Society for Psychical Research on November 13, 1994, saying: 'The children had just made their first Holy Communion. Keith's dad took a series of photos. On this one at the side of Melanie is a hand with a ring. No one [underlined twice] else was on the altar at the time. The hand is on the negative. A professional photographer has looked at the photo and negative and cannot explain…'

In fact, no one has been able to explain this image. I definitely discount fraud because there would be no motive for doing such a thing, and a double exposure would not be possible in this case. The likelihood of someone standing behind the girl, perhaps to adjust her headdress or veil, can also be thrown out, because he or she would be very tightly squashed against the rail around the altar and would have disturbed the children. Perhaps part of the same wooden rail has been somehow distorted by the girl's veil? As always, developing chemicals can cause glitches in negatives and prints, but these are usually blurs rather than such a comparatively well defined image. So that takes us back to a proud father on the day of his daughter's first Communion…doesn't it?

'at the side of Melanie is a hand with a ring'

Spirit Head Joins Party Table

LOCATION: Hotel Vierjahreszeiten, Maurach, Austria
DATE: 1988

Psychical researcher Maurice Grosse is adamant about this disturbing photograph, saying, '…fraud can be completely ruled out. The circumstances under which the photograph was taken would not have lent itself to the necessary technical set up to obtain such a picture, even indeed if it was possible at all.' So, who is the oversized woman, with just her head and shoulders on the table? How did she get there? No one yet knows. But here is what was said to have happened. On the last night of a group vacation, four couples met for a farewell party and were joined by three other people. Mr. Todd set up his camera (Canon T50 with Fuji 100 colour film) on a nearby table using a delayed-action ten-second timer and returned to his seat. The shutter clicked and the film wound on, but the flash did not operate (see near right). He reset the camera and took another shot with the flash. No one took much notice when the pictures were developed until one of the subjects, suddenly noticed the outsized head (see top right). The photographic department of Leicester University did not believe it to be a double exposure, and neither did the Society for Psychical Research nor the Royal Photographic Society. Despite the photograph having received publicity nobody has claimed to be the face in the picture. It's said to remain a mystery. Certainly one mystery is why the group of women on the right seemed to have moved seats, so the head conceals none of them. But if this was a deliberate double exposure, how was the 'ghost' woman so precisely placed between the other heads in the group?

'who is the oversized woman, with just her head and shoulders on the table?'

The Spectre at the Organ

LOCATION: Unknown
DATE: 1939

Any fan of horror movies knows there is quite a tradition of spooky organ music being heard when no one else is supposed to be around to play it. This is one of the very few photographs known of an actual 'spectral' player, and its story includes some of the best-known followers of Spiritualism from the first half of the 20th century. Mrs. Bertha Harris was well known as a medium in Spiritualist circles, and Lady Conan Doyle introduced her to the psychic photographer William Hope. Mrs. Harris told the psychic researcher, Cyril Permutt, she obtained the best psychic photographs (of spirits who appeared while she was in a séance) if a man and a woman worked together. So Mrs. Harris and Mr. Hope teamed up and the results were splendid. It is not known where they obtained the picture, although the organ looks of a size that would only be found in a church or a hall. With the involvement of Lady Conan Doyle and by inference Sir Arthur, it's difficult to believe the creator of Sherlock Holmes' fanatically forensic mind could be tricked.

Yet the spirit photographs of William Hope have been widely discredited and an association with Mrs. Harris, clearly raises the possibility of collaboration and deceit, perhaps as simple as double exposures. But, just because it is possible to fake photographs of this kind it should not be thought every example is fraudulent. This could be a genuine photograph of a ghostly organist. Couldn't it?

'an actual "spectural" player, and its story includes some of the best followers of spiritualism'

Headless Torso on the Dee

LOCATION: River Dee, Chester, Cheshire, England
DATE: 1994

First you must discount the name of the showboat; in 1994 Diana, Princess of Wales, was still alive and so there's no clue or message from her spirit here. The *Lady Diana* showboat was at its mooring when Mr. and Mrs. Lavender took a snap of her, during a day trip to Chester. When they had the prints developed they were surprised to see the seemingly headless torso and it was duly printed in the *Liverpool Daily Post* on August 17, 1994. Some explanations offered are that the head of the person could simply be bent forward looking at something, that the torso was later superimposed, and that it might simply be a tailor's dummy.

'is it not curious that no one else who was around ever came forward'

These explanations all have flaws. The bend of the neck would have been unnaturally acute to achieve this effect and superimposition of this quality could only have been achieved with computer technology not widely available in 1994. Anyway, the Lavenders claimed neither knowledge nor equipment. That leaves the dummy. Perhaps this is what it was and the Lavenders either have or have not known all the time? But is it not curious that no one else who was around ever came forward to say they saw it too? Then there's the puzzle of which way the headless body is facing. It's generally been thought of as a man, facing away. However, there is also the possibility that the figure is that of a woman. Perhaps the clue is in the showboat after all, and the torso is a theatrical prop put there to have some fun. If so, I wish someone would get in touch and tell me.

Black Figure in Covent Garden

LOCATION: Covent Garden Piazza, London, England
DATE: December 31, 1989

Mr. Webb took this picture of his family, framing his daughter in the foreground and with Mrs. Webb following behind with the push-chair. The legless apparition floating through the scene was not intended to be part of this family group. The couple sent the photograph to the Society for Psychical Research in January 1990. Mrs. Webb says there was no one next to them, that the barrier and the white car made it very difficult for anyone to have passed by them, and also pointed out that there appeared to be an unnatural slant to the strange figure.

'well known for wearing black because she claimed it made her stronger'

Dr. Vernon Harrison, photographic expert of the Society for Psychical Research said 'The whole disposition of the figure seems an impossible one to me for a person in the act of running across the front of the push chair and the dreamy expression on her face does not seem consonant with physical exertion.' He also suggested thoughtography as a possible explanation. After the photograph was published in *Unexplained Magazine* Maurice Grosse (Society for Psychical Research) received a letter from a security guard who used to work at Covent Garden. He said he recognized the girl, explaining she was well known for wearing black because she claimed it made her stronger and that she dabbled in black magic. Grosse replied but did not receive a response. Take another, cool look. Isn't the 'unnatural slant' of the girl just the involuntary head dip we make when we suddenly find ourself in someone else's camera shot? That certainly makes it possible her legs are behind the post. And isn't her dreamy expression the perfectly common 'I'm not impressed' face-set of the young? Up to you.

A Gnarled Hand at her Throat

LOCATION: Essex or Sussex, England
DATE: 1991

Whose is the gnarled hand that intrudes on this picture of three schoolfriends? Kelley Jackson was 12 at the time and says that when she took this picture there was no one else present and no one noticed anything strange. It was three years later in 1994 that she wrote to the Society for Psychical Research: 'We found the hand had arthritic fingers and it couldn't have been anybody from our school because our uniform is red and the sleeve is blue.' That's a puzzling thing to say about an aged adult who surely wouldn't wear the same colour as the pupils and who could also have been someone employed at the castle. Kelley first described the location as 'a castle in Sussex', but later on in her letter she called it 'Mountfiget Castle' [sic]. If she meant 'Mountfichet' castle, this is in Stansted, Essex and not in Sussex.

> 'it couldn't have been anybody from our school'

This is a troubling image but it contains some illogicalities. When I look carefully at the photograph it becomes clear to me the expression of the girl with the hand at her throat is different from the others. Her two companions are smiling but she is gritting her teeth, exactly as you would if someone suddenly laid a hand on you, even in passing, and she is, perhaps, starting to protest. I don't think it important that Kelley is confused about which castle she was in. Castle names aren't very important when you are 12 or 15 years old. But many much older photographers and their subjects famously don't notice or remember fleeting events or changes that are then recorded on their film. I think Kelley and her friends were having such a good time they simply didn't notice what really did happen. If there is not such a rational explanation then this becomes a very real anomaly, and one that is certainly worth exploring in much greater depth.

Execution on the Underground

LOCATION: Bakerloo Line Underground train, London, England
DATE: 1985

Why would Bruno Richard Hauptmann, executed for the kidnap and murder of the Lindbergh baby in 1936, appear in the window of a London Underground train? That's what Mrs. Woo needed to know. She thought she had simply taken a snap of her nephew from Malaysia, who badly wanted a picture of himself on the Underground. Yet when the picture was developed, there seemed to be the partial picture of a man in an electric chair with sparks coming from his hands, just above her nephew's head. For some reason, Mrs. Woo recognized the likeness as similar to the waxwork in Madame Tussaud's famous 'Chamber of Horrors'. Sure enough, the waxwork was identical (minus the sparks), but there were no posters advertising the museum at the time, and anyway, the picture was taken between stations, so a poster visible through the window can be discounted. Subsequently a medium confirmed it was Hauptmann that Mrs. Woo had captured, and claimed he was saying he was innocent of the crime for which he had been executed.

'he was saying he was innocent of the crime for which he had been executed'

The lighting of this photograph is curiously shallow, with no apparent flash reflection in the window or details of the seats in which they are sitting, not even between their clearly lit legs. Mrs. Woo's obvious belief in the paranormal means thoughtography could be a plausible explanation for this real conundrum. I have to say, though, that a plausible explanation of any kind for this picture, including a paranormal one, remains intriguingly unknown.

Apparition at Arundel Altar

LOCATION: St. Nicholas' Church, Arundel, Sussex, England
DATE: 1940

A ghostly vigil at the altar or a photographic error? What gives away a double exposure, whether intended or not, is faint remainders of other parts of the second picture, surrounding the main subject. This type of occurence seems especially likely at a time of such little photographic sophistication as World War II. Could there really have been a carved white structure stuck so tightly between the right-hand pews and the altar rail? Are they part of the emanation, or clues to trick photography? In 1989 computer enhancement was alleged to have found the picture was probably 'a multiple exposure of a woman ascending the altar steps with a taper and lighting one of the altar candles'. This makes sense for paranormal sceptics, but less sense for photography sceptics. Did anyone really have such good computers in 1989?

This church in the grounds of Arundel Castle was built on the site of a Norman priory, and the adjoining Fitzalan Chapel, originally part of the same church, also has a tradition of being haunted. Ghosts are commonly seen in places where emotions can be extreme. It thus makes sense to learn pubs are a frequent place for paranormal sightings. So churches, where everything from baptisms to weddings and funerals are held, are prime sites. This is a classic ghost picture exactly where you expect to see one. Is this why it is suspicious, or does that make it curiously reassuring?

'Ghosts are commonly seen in places where emotions can be extreme'

The Uninvited Guest

LOCATION: Zoetermeer, Holland
DATE: 1994?

There is a rather distinct mystery about the ephemeral image seen in both these photographs sent to the Society for Psychical Research. Uncommonly, there are more than just two photographs known, and they have each been taken from dramatically different points of view. Thus, because the unidentified phenomenon is seen so diversely, there seems no possibility of it being a curiosity of light or of it being a camera fault. The number of images and range of viewpoints, which must have been taken over a period of time, make highly unusual circumstances and create one of the most intriguing cases of all. The same person was said to have taken both these pictures, using the same camera. No one else in the church appeared to be aware of the apparition, as you can see for yourself.

On the right of the altar there is certainly a shape. It might be thought human, perhaps with an outstretched arm and head covering. What do you think it is? One explanation could be pareidolia, the self-protective trait of the human brain, which translates unknown shapes into something familiar, to calm our fears. Rise above this and refuse to see something recognizable if you want, but then you have to ask yourself what it might be if not once a human being; there is no rule to say what a ghost should look like. It would be fascinating to track down the bride and groom and ask if either had a close, but dead, relative whom they wished had been at the wedding. Or whom they had dreaded being at the wedding, yet who unexpectedly turned up.

'there seems no possibility of it being a curiosity of light'

The Spirit of Old Nanna

LOCATION: Unknown
DATE: 1991

Two-year-old Greg Sheldon Maxwell is obviously entranced by something he can see. These moments of rapture happened whenever he began pointing to part of a room and saying, 'Old Nanna's here'. But Old Nanna, his great grandmother, was dead, and no one else could see a thing. The boy's moments of classic transfixion were then photographed with the result you can see, but the mist was only revealed on the print; again no one else in the room saw anything.

The story sort of makes sense paranormally, yet there is not enough verifiable fact to support the appearance and photographing of a spirit. We don't know who the photographer was, or what was shown in any other pictures taken. Did the boy often sit with his fingers folded together, as children do when they first learn to pray, or only when he was experiencing something wonderful? If the picture is fraudulent then the misty cloud should be explainable but it's far too big and dense to be, say, cigarette smoke. Neither is there anything to suggest a human form but, of course, what the boy saw and what we are permitted to see could be quite different.

'moments of rapture happened whenever he began pointing to part of a room and saying "Old Nanna's here"'

A Ghostly Dinner Intruder?

LOCATION: St Mary's Guildhall, Coventry, England,
DATE: 22 January 1985

You would expect St Mary's Guildhall in Coventry to be haunted. Built in the 14th century, it was prison to the doomed Mary, Queen of Scots, and was Henry VI's Lancastrian headquarters during the bloody Wars of the Roses. At times of famine, its kitchens fed starving weavers. And then there's the mystery of its extraordinary survival during Coventry's terrible bomb blitz in the World War II. Did the Guildhall have some supernatural protection?

In this photograph of a Coventry Freeman's dinner there definitely seems to be a curious figure dominating the top of the left hand table, with a white hood and its face hidden in shadow. The figure is large and appears slightly apart from the other diners on the table. Even allowing for the effects of lighting, the mysterious figure appears to be wearing clothes from another era. Lord Mayor Walter Brandish was convinced there was no-one who was dressed like that there and instigated a further investigation. But nobody seems to have seen, or owned up to being the unknown intruder.

'the mysterious figure appears to be wearing clothes from another era'

Now look again. Is there really an intruder? The diners are saying Grace and with bowing their heads and then sitting down it would be easy not to notice someone who perhaps came in a wrong door, stood still for Grace, and then dashed away. However, count the glasses and you'll see there is the same number as the guests, including the mystery diner. But where is their chair? All the other diners on the table are standing behind their own chair.

The Forgotten Prisoner of Newgate

LOCATION: Old Newgate Prison, City of London, England
DATE: 1988

Newgate Prison in the City of London was infamous, the most feared lock-up in all England for almost one thousand years. Until 1868 condemned men and women were hung outside its walls, while the public watched, and from then until 1901 the hangings took place inside. Today, The Old Bailey, England's premier courts of justice, stands on the site. But, beneath the ground, some of the cells still exist, cells where starving, neglected men, women, and children lived in unspeakable misery. In 1988 Lars Thomas was on a guided tour of the basement of the Viaduct Inn, built over some of these former cells. He was certain no one stood in front of him when he took the picture but as you can see, someone or something did manifest itself, with a head craned up as though looking for an ever-impossible escape.

'beneath the ground, some of the cells still exist, cells where starving, neglected men, women and children lived in unspeakable misery'

Using daylight film when the lighting was from tungsten-filament bulbs causes the curious red tone of the photograph. This is a common occurrence familiar to most photographers. So that's not mysterious. What has to be considered is if this unexpected image really is, or once was, a man. Is the neck puzzlingly too thin, and is that a bald head or a flat cap? Those answers might be there if the image was less blurred. That's if there is an answer. No use saying, 'If these walls could speak…' Perhaps they have spirits among them anxious to be seen and to speak?

FAMOUS MYSTERIES

If just one of these mysterious shots genuinely shows someone or something from outside current understanding, the scientific world would have to change or adapt many of its long-held theories. And so would we. That's why these images are so very famous internationally.

Some of these photographs have been analyzed for more than a century. Each one still prompts discussion, sometimes heated, for and against its validity. Suggestions that the image caught by security cameras at Belgrave Hall is simply an out-of-focus oak leaf seem plausible. But this was caught on videotape, and there is no sign of the 'leaf' coming into or out of the frame. Whatever it is just appears, remains for a few seconds, and then disappears. That's why it's still being talked about in the committees of the psychical research societies. Examples from the USA and Australia are particularly interesting because they take us away from the suspicious settings of the ivy-clad country houses, old churches, and ruined castles of England. Yet, if the paranormal is a reality it must be seen in every country, and rather than being surprised to find the photograph taken in a graveyard of Chicago, we should be comforted. If, that is, we believe in the paranormal.

Of course, one needs to accept the testimony of the photographers as a starting point and hope they are not either lying outright or being economical with the truth. Does someone know the living identity of the woman on the tombstone in Bachelor's Grove, Chicago? Does someone know the technical secrets of the triple shot of the boy without a shirt? The Tulip Staircase, taken by

Canadians at Greenwich, London, has probably appeared in more books than any other, and still hasn't been satisfactorily explained. It, like others you will see, shows a particular image of an apparition, in ghostly white drapery. But we still don't know for sure what we are seeing.

As you will have realized by now, there have been 'ghost' photographs claimed since the beginnings of photography. Hundreds have been sent to psychical researchers over the years, most of which are easily explainable.

But others are not. In recent years the advent of digital cameras, cameras on mobile phones, the ease of photo-manipulation and the internet have vastly proliferated the number of anomalous photographs that crop up, but also make it harder to believe that they are genuine. It's all too easy to assume that some sort of digital manipulation has taken place. The photographs in this chapter have stood up to scrutiny. They have been published repeatedly, investigated by psychical researchers, and yet still haven't given up their secrets.

The Spectre on the Staircase

LOCATION: Raynham Hall, Norfolk, England
DATE: September 19, 1936

There was a tradition of hauntings at Raynham Hall and, most unusually, evidence of the same seems to have been caught on film. At the commission of *Country Life* two reporters (Captain Provand and Indre Shira) were sent to Raynham Hall to photograph the house. Towards the end of the session Indre Shira noticed a spectral figure descending the stairs and he asked Captain Provand to quickly photograph it. The end result was the photograph reproduced here, which is generally believed to be the ghost of Dorothy Walpole (d. 1729) the second wife of Charles 2nd Viscount Townshend.

'it was seen by the naked eye before being photographed'

This image is one of the most famous to appear in print and it has been investigated at length by several people since it was taken. C. V. C. Herbert of the Society for Psychical Research discovered further details about the camera used and the lens and setting, and Harry Price and Nandor Fodor, well known investigators, believed it to be genuine. More recently in the 1960s Dennis Bardens (Ghost Club) was also impressed with its veracity. The barrister Alan Murdie has cast doubt concerning its genuineness in *Fortean Times* October 2006, but Peter Meadows, in charge of manuscripts at the Cambridge University Library, has found other photographic evidence that challenges some of his statements.

The evidence in favour of this being a 'ghostly' image includes the fact that it was seen by the naked eye before being photographed – the reporters appeared to be genuine – experienced researchers believed the negative to be genuine and a tradition of haunting was known at the house. The evidence against its veracity is that there appear to be inconsistencies in the photo on the stair rail and some people believe it to be impossible to photograph paranormal events and especially ghosts. Let the viewer decide.

White Lady on the Tombstone

LOCATION: Bachelor's Grove Cemetery, Chicago, Illinois, USA
DATE: August 10, 1991

Some people believe the White Lady of Bachelor's Grove is the ghost of Mrs. Rogers, searching mournfully for the grave of her dead baby or sitting in communion with its spirit. An unnamed infant is buried close by. This image by Mari Huff was taken near the south entrance of the graveyard and shows a saddened, somewhat slumped woman, sitting on the well known tombstone with a checkered pattern carved into it. The strange white mist around her feet is said to be the natural debris of leaves, grass and twigs affected by the type of film used.

'searching mournfully for the grave of her dead baby'

There is a long tradition of apparitions, strange blue orbs, and other paranormal phenomena in this graveyard, and it was the site of a tragic murder. In 1991 the Ghost Research Society mounted a vigil, using black and white infrared film to photograph the location. The Society states very clearly that no one was in the shot when it was taken. Even if someone did get into the photo and rested there for a while, it's hard to explain why the far leg is so transparent and the face is so shapeless. One notion is that the face has been tampered with and the leg was moved into that position during the exposure, thus not allowing the film to fix it accurately. But once again, cool reasoning must be used. Why would the Society fiddle with or lie about a subject they take so seriously?

Did Freddy Jackson Return?

LOCATION: Probably HMS *Daedalus*, Lee-on-Solent, Hampshire, England
DATE: 1919

Did air-mechanic Freddy Jackson return from the dead to be in this photograph? In 1919 the Royal Naval Air Service, later the Fleet Air Arm, was established at Lee-on-Solent, now RAF Cranwell. Probably serving on HMS *Daedalus*, this photograph of fellow airmen from his squadron was taken two days after a plane's propeller killed Freddy. Look closely behind the left ear of the fourth airman from the left, on the top row. The close-up clearly shows another man's face, and many of his friends are said to have recognized it as Freddy. Spookily, the picture was taken on the same day as his funeral; perhaps Freddy didn't know he was dead, and turned up for the photograph as arranged.

'taken on the same day as his funeral; perhaps Freddy didn't know he was dead'

Sir Victor Goddard, a retired RAF officer who was present brought the picture to public attention first, but this was not until 1975, more than half a century after it was taken. A number of other sources have published it subsequently, but none provides concrete evidence about how the 'extra' image was identified, or by whom. This is a typical case where the explanation might not be something paranormal. It may simply be another man making an appearance during the exposure, or one of the airman moving. But it does appear to be a different face to the man from behind whom he is peering – and unlike everyone else in the picture, he doesn't appear to be wearing a cap. An interesting photograph worthy of inclusion in a collection of this type. Not least because it might jog the memory of similar photographs from other private collections that are waiting to be examined and explained.

The Girl Who Returned

LOCATION: Town Hall, Wem, Shropshire, England
DATE: November 19, 1995

Is this Jane Churm, accused of burning down the Wem Town Hall in 1677? This seems to be one paranormal explanation for this extraordinarily dramatic photograph. Tony O'Rahilly took the shot as Wem Town Hall was being gutted by a fire. Because of the intense heat, police and firemen had stopped people getting close to the flames. This meant he had to photograph the building from the other side of the road, using a 200mm telescopic lens. Nobody remembers seeing anyone in the blaze, which was so intense that survival would not have been possible. The face has never been formally identified, so who is she, and what is this girl in the old-fashioned bonnet trying to communicate to us today?

'was she still frantically trying to communicate something?'

The photograph was sent to the Association for the Scientific Study of Anomalous Phenomena, who in turn sent it to the photographic expert, Dr. Vernon Harrison. He declared that neither the picture nor the negative had been doctored, but that it might have been produced by a trick of light causing an optical illusion. Some of the architectural details need explaining, but it's an arresting combination. A pretty girl and two fires on the same historic site: just the sort of dramatic coincidence you might expect in a Hollywood thriller. Or, it could be true that Jane Churm did return on the night the Town Hall burned down again. Was she still frantically trying to communicate something about the original blaze, almost 320 years earlier?

Manifestation in a Security Camera

LOCATION: Belgrave Hall Museum, Leicester, England
DATE: December 23, 1998

At 4:48 am precisely this spectral image suddenly appeared on a security camera outside Belgrave Hall Museum. It remained still for five seconds and then instantly disappeared without any blurring of fall or flight. At the same time there was a digital timing malfunction, as though time was being suddenly displaced. Yet mechanical failure can be ruled out. This was a new security system, tested only one month earlier and subsequently retested. The site of the alleged apparition is especially relevant, because the 18th-century hall is supposedly built on crossroads used as an unhallowed graveyard for those not welcome in consecrated ground. And there had long been claims of a ghostly figure appearing inside the hall as well as scary sounds and untraceable smells.

In 1999 the press took up the possibility of a Belgrave Hall haunting, and explanations generated included the spirit of a Victorian lady, a plastic bag, a blown leaf, insects, and raindrops on the lens of the camera, but there was no rain and no strong wind on the night. The Association for the Scientific Study of Anomalous Phenomena undertook two vigils there without reporting any unusual phenomena. They also tried to replicate the image by using leaves thrown into the air. To them and to the museum staff this appeared to be the most likely explanation. But they had not considered the digital timing malfunction and Maurice Grosse of the Society for Psychical Research said he was convinced 'the security camera captured a manifestation of psychic activity'. No truly convincing explanation has ever been given.

'the 18th-century hall is supposedly built on crossroads used as an unhallowed graveyard'

The Observer at Corroboree Rock

LOCATION: Corroboree Rock, Alice Springs, Northern Territory, Australia
DATE: 1959

Few occasions can be more sacred or spiritual than an Aboriginal corroboree, when rhythmic percussion, didgeridoo music, traditional songs, and repetitive dancing create tribal unity under night skies. Corroboree Rock is 100 miles west of Alice Springs and the chosen site for other important rites. There is little familiar about the figure, who seems to be dressed in an all-encasing robe and tight-fitting helmet, not what you would normally choose in the stifling temperatures at the very heart of Australia.

'a bizarre solution other than the paranormal occurs to me'

Even more puzzling is what he is holding and looking at so intently. Some sort of camera perhaps? This is one case where a bizarre solution other than the paranormal occurs to me. Is this someone from another planet, who allowed himself to be seen? If it is simply an unidentified human, the unique photographs he took that day have have never been seen. So, who or what was the silent observer at Corroboree Rock? Contentiously, I should add that a church minister took this shot, it is usual to think a minister is above suspicion when providing details of the paranormal, but it is naïve to believe that every case reported has been without inaccuracies, intentional or otherwise.

Who is the Back Seat Passenger?

LOCATION: Ipswich, Suffolk, England
DATE: March 22, 1959

Mabel Chinnery and her husband had just visited her mother's grave. She decided to use the last shot in her camera to photograph her husband sitting alone in the car. Mrs. Chinnery was convinced the developed image showed another figure, her dead mother, with light reflected in her spectacles, sitting in her favourite spot in the car. No one should doubt her sincerity but perhaps she put a human face on to something unfamiliar and otherwise unsettling.

> '**Powerful emotions could have let Mrs. Chinnery create a thought photograph of her departed mother**'

In this case, the possibility of a double exposure must be considered. On the right is what at first seems to be the door pillar of the far side of the car, but isn't it much too far forward, aren't the windows too big, and does the curved right side look like a tree trunk? The supposed mother's figure looks unnaturally close to the front seat and couldn't be sitting on the back seat. Even Mr. Chinnery's face seems too big. Was the window open or closed? Before this can be accepted as a genuine paranormal image, these points have to be rationalized. Until then it's just as likely Mrs. Chinnery's emotional state confused her about the last shot, famously easy to expose twice. Yet many believe the same powerful emotions could have let Mrs. Chinnery create a thought photograph of her departed mother, and that other unexplained phenomena are simply a result of this imagery from another realm. This would then be an extraordinary example of an unidentified power of the human mind.

Apparition at Hampton Court Palace

LOCATION: Hampton Court Palace, Middlesex, England
DATE: October 7, 2003

Security staff heard alarms, activated by fire doors, which should always have been kept closed. They checked the CCTV footage to find out what had happened and were astonished to see this skeletal figure in a long, hooded cloak emerge from behind the doors. Romantic, redbrick Hampton Court Palace appears to sit serenely by the gentle Thames River. But its history is violent, the scene of much turbulence, betrayal, and death. No wonder there are tales of more than one royal haunting: the most likely candidates would be two of Henry VIII's wives; Anne Boleyn executed in 1536 or Catherine Howard, beheaded in 1542. Even Henry himself is supposed to have been seen, as well as a sad pageboy from the time of Charles II.

> '**No wonder there are tales of more than one royal haunting**'

There's absolutely no denying the presence of a figure and that the clothing seems authentically historical. To me it looks more like a determined man than the spirit of a restless queen of Tudor England. The sceptical Richard Wiseman, professor of psychology, University of Hertfordshire, says that if this were a genuine apparition the spectre would be a 'significant discovery'. He's more likely to go along with those who say it was a tourist in a costume who was lost, or a member of staff who dressed up to do this, for publicity's sake. But the testimony of all the palace staff denies this and they stress that these doors are in a part of the building off limits to the public. Neither has been identified, if that were so. Experiments at the palace have shown genuinely colder areas associated with alleged haunting are actually cooled by drafts from concealed doors. What do you think? Is there always a logical answer, or could this be the genuine image of an apparition on film, one of the most rare things in the world?

Spectre Priest at Woodford Altar

LOCATION: St. Mary the Virgin, Woodford, Northamptonshire, England
DATE: July 1964

Two years after it was taken, Gordon Carroll and his friend David Hadsell were astonished to find that this photograph included the image of what looks like someone in deep meditation before the altar of St. Mary the Virgin's church. This is not seen in the next frame he took. Gordon was only 16 at the time, but took great care about his photographs, using a tripod for this shot to eliminate any camera shake.

'a fleeting spectral instance, usually hidden from our sight'

It's very easy for sceptics to claim a cleaner might have been at work or that a passing vicar might have knelt there briefly, although a short-sleeved white shift tied at the waist seems unlikely clerical attire. Gordon and David were both convinced no one had approached the altar while they were taking photographs, and two heads are much more believable than one. To support their veracity and honesty the local vicar gave them both a pristine character reference and Agfa (the film manufacturers) said there were no traces of a double exposure, and 'no flaw in the actual film or fault in development'.

But there is a very plausible explanation, if you believe in the paranormal. St. Mary the Virgin's former priest, the Reverend Basil Eversley Owen, had died only the year before and he was well known for spending time in devotion on this very spot. You can only speculate about whether he had returned, or if he had never left and the teenagers captured a fleeting spectral instance, usually hidden from our sight.

The Haunted Doorway

LOCATION: Probably England
DATE: 1920s

This is the classic image of what most people would think a ghost should look like, a semi-transparent shrouded figure. Hollywood has certainly done everything in its power to reinforce such expectations. This photograph is generally known among those interested in the paranormal as Spencer's Ghost, but only because it was sent to psychical researcher John Spencer, some time in 1993. Spencer was sufficiently intrigued by the picture to investigate and even consulted a medium, who suggested the thatched building (more a barn than a cottage, perhaps) might be in a village near Mottram, Greater Manchester. Spencer added: 'While a number of methods could be suggested for faking the "ghost", inquiries made of various photographers suggest that whatever the apparition might or might not be it was genuinely in front of the camera when the photograph was taken. The mystery still remains.'

The dearth of information means the authenticity of this photograph will always be dubious, not least because most people are suspicious of the dramatic drapery, when by far the majority of investigations of the Society for Psychical Research have been sightings of what looked like real people in real clothes. Modern computers are constant proof of how much a photograph can lie, but they can also prove the reverse. One day, technology could well tell us this apparition is exactly what it seems to be: a genuine paranormal presence.

> 'it was genuinely in front of the camera when the photograph was taken'

Triple Echo of the Future

LOCATION: Virginia, USA
DATE: 1950s

Accidental triple exposures are virtually unheard of, but such a rarity is an outside possibility here. The stories that come with this startling picture certainly make you think something else might have happened. Sam Watkins thought he was taking a picture of his dog, but when he developed the Polaroid print he found three ghostly images of his brother instead. What's more, just a few days later, a passing car hit his brother and he was dressed exactly like this when it happened.

'just a few days later a passing car hit his brother'

Polaroid cameras were notorious for taking double-exposures if you accidentally pressed the button twice in quick enough succession. Yet, look again at the boy who was allegedly involved in a car accident a few days later. None of the images are noticeably sharper than the others and with multi-exposures the first one or the last one is usually clearer. And what's going on with the shadows? The two on the left go one way, and the one on the right goes the other. A slippage of time might be thought to have caused this anomaly and to be a warning of tragedy to come. Often, the anomalous explanation is easier to accept. Until I see and hear an explanation of how a triple image could have been faked on a Polaroid, my mind is open, but leaning towards a paranormal occurrence.

Spooky Giant at the Altar

LOCATION: Church of Christ the Consoler, Skelton-cum-Newby, Yorkshire, England
DATE: July or August 1954

When a respectable vicar says he took a photograph like this in his own church, you have to at least accept that he thinks he's telling the truth. The Reverend Kenneth F. Lord said it was a summer evening, about 6 pm, and that no one else was in the church except for a single friend. That abnormally tall figure on the steps to the altar is certainly not the friend he's talking about! His purpose was to photograph the altar and not until the film was developed did he notice this curious ghoul.

Even if you accept the possibility of accidental but somehow overlooked or forgotten double exposure, you have to ask why a vicar would choose to photograph someone dressed like they were wearing a Hallowe'en spook costume, and at the wrong time of year. The mask looks like sheeting rather than something vaporous and spiritual. And on second look, the apparition might not be as tall as first appears, but could be standing on the top step, the robe artfully draped and arranged over the other two. This is clearly not what you would expect from something supposedly without substance. But as I've asked before, what should a ghost look like? If this is as genuine a photograph as the Reverend Lord believes, it is truly one of the most remarkable examples of an apparition ever recorded.

'one of the most remarkable examples of an apparition ever recorded'

The Tulip Staircase Mystery

LOCATION: The Queen's House, Greenwich, London, England
DATE: June 19, 1966

The Tulip Staircase was barred to visitors so the Reverend and Mrs. Hardy from Canada took a photograph to study later. They had come especially to learn more about the exquisite architectural details of The Queen's House in Greenwich. Queen Anne commissioned it in the height of 1616 fashion from the architect Inigo Jones. It was her escape from the general disinterest in her by her husband, King James I of England and VI of Scotland. The staircase was entrancing, unique for its beautiful tulip motifs on the curved flight up to the next floor, and they were thrilled they at least had a photograph. But they got more than they expected, for the print showed the straining image of someone in grey robes, perhaps a monk, clinging to the balustrade, and seeming to want to drag itself up the staircase. But to what?

A thorough appraisal of the photograph was made, including interviews of the Hardys who confirmed nobody else was on the stairs. A Ghost Club vigil produced no conclusive evidence of a haunting despite inexplicable sounds and impressions being noted. The National Maritime Museum's photographer Brian Tremain did replicate a similar photograph using a member of staff on the staircase and a long exposure. But his success does not mean the Hardys were hoaxers; there is every reason to believe a man of the cloth and his wife about something so fundamental to their personal belief as spirits. So, we are left with a dilemma. Who or what was trying to ascend the Tulip Staircase and why did it choose to appear only to the Reverend and Mrs. Hardy? It's a mystery we

> 'the print showed the straining image of someone in grey robes'

Bibliography

Annals Of Psychical Science (London, 1913).

Apraxine, Pierre, Canguilhem, Denis, Chéroux, Clément, Fischer, Andreas and Schmit, Sophie (eds.), *The Perfect Medium: Photography and the Occult* (Yale University Press, 2004).

Baraduc, H., *The Human Soul: Its Movements, Its Lights, and the Iconography Of the Fluid Invisible* (London, 1913).

Barbanell, Maurice, 'Scientist Took 44 Photos of Spirit Form', *Noah's Ark*, 3, 50 (September 1994), 9-12.

The British Journal of Photography (1982/1983).

Carroll, Robert Todd, *The Skeptic's Dictionary*, (John Wiley & Sons, 2003).

Dash, Mike, 'Whatever Happened to Spirit Photography?', *Fortean Times*, 123 (June 1999).

Doyle, Sir Arthur Conan, *The Coming of the Fairies* (Hodder & Stoughton, 1922).

Earwicker, Simon, 'The Witness Camera', *ASSAP News*, 77 (July 2000), 4–5.

Eisenbud, J., *The World of Ted Serios: 'Thoughtographic' Studies of an Extraordinary Mind* (William Morrow Company, 1967).

Fielding, Everard, *Sittings with Eusapia Palladino & Other Studies* (New York University Books, 1963).

Fodor, Nandor, *Encyclopaedia of Psychic Science* (Arthurs Press Limited, London, 1933).

Gettings, Fred, *Ghosts in Photographs: The Extraordinary Story of Spirit Photography* (Outlet, 1978).

Haining, Peter, *Ghosts: The Illustrated History* (Sidgwick & Jackson, London,1974).

Houghton, Georgina, *Chronicles of the Photographs of Spiritual Beings and Phenomena Invisible to the Material Eye Interblended With Personal Narrative* (London, 1882).

Into the Unknown, (Reader's Digest, 1982).

Jones, R., *Walking Haunted London* (New Holland Publishers, London, 1999).

Journal of the Society for Psychical Research, 59, 830 (1993).

Krauss, R., *Beyond Light and Shadow* (Nazraeli Press, Munich, 1994).

Lamar Keene, M. and Spraggett, Allen, *The Psychic Mafia* (Dell Publishing, 1976).

Marriott, William, *Pearson's Magazine* (1910).

McEwan, Graham J., *Haunted Churches of England* (Robert Hale, London, 1989).

Mumler, W. M., *Personal Experiences of William H. Mumler in Spirit Photography* (Colby & Rich, 1875).

Pagan Dawn (The Pagan Federation, London).

Parker, D. and Parker, J., *Atlas of the Supernatural* (Prentice Hall Press, New York, 1990).

Permutt, Cyril, *Beyond the Spectrum* (Patrick Stephens, Cambridge, 1983).

Picknett, Lynn, *The Encyclopaedia of the Paranormal* (Guild Publishing, London, 1990).

Princess Mary, *Princess Mary's Gift Book* (Hodder & Stoughton, London, 1917).

'Proceedings of the Parapsychology Association', 5 (1968).

Randi, James, *The Supernatural A-Z* (Headline Book Publishing, London 1995).

Townsend, Maurice, 'How To Take Anomalous Photos', *Anomaly*, 38 (May 2005), 2–15.

Underwood, Peter, *The Ghost Hunter's Guide* (Javelin Books, London, 1988).

Underwood, Peter, *Ghosts and How To See Them* (BCA, London, 1993).

Underwood, Peter, *Nights in Haunted Houses* (Headline, London, 1994).

Willin, M. J., *Music, Witchcraft and the Paranormal* (Melrose, Ely, 2005).

Wilson, Ian, *In Search of Ghosts* (Headline Book Publishing Company, London, 1995) 45–46.

Winchester, Alf, 'Why the Spheres Are Invisible – Spirit Photographs', *Noah's Ark*, 4, 57 (April 1995).

Index

Numbers in *italic* refer to illustrations

Acknowledgments

I would like to dedicate this book to the memory of Maurice Grosse whose enthusiastic work in collecting photographs of anomalous phenomena made the task of presenting new material considerably less daunting.

Thanking people is a thankless task since one is almost guaranteed to upset someone by their omission or even inclusion. So I start with a big 'sorry' to any of you who I have placed in this deplorable position! Neither do I wish to bore the reader with an enormous list of my ancestors or beyond. In these days of political correctness I must also stress that the order of appreciation does not imply an hierarchy of gratitude. My interest in ghosts and allied phenomena would not have come into being if I had not been inspired by the late John Mitchell in York and the many works of the author Peter Underwood. My approach to the paranormal was guided by my friend and mentor, again alas, the late Professor Bob Morris at the Parapsychology Unit at Edinburgh University. During the search for photographs of ghosts I was helped by friends such as Steve Hulford who tracked down some of the images and Karen Patel who sorted out piles of references and stopped me tearing my last few remaining hairs out when things went wrong! I must also thank John Kirkpatrick for providing the glorious music that inspired me as I wrote and re-wrote the script deep into the night. As the Honorary Archive Officer to the Society for Psychical Research I was able to access many photographs in their collection and I am very grateful to this fine organization. Of course, I must thank my publishers for allowing me to produce this book and especially Neil Baber and Louise Clark who provided support throughout the venture. Finally, thank you reader for buying this copy and hopefully thousands more to give to your friends, family, neighbours, doctor, dentist, local policeman, school teachers, psychiatrist, lawyer, bank manager, plumber, clergyman, pets, garden gnomes etc. Thank you!

Picture Credits

The photographs used in this book have come from many sources and acknowledgment has been made wherever possible. If images have been used without due credit or acknowledgment, through no fault of our own, apologies are offered. If notified, the publisher will be pleased to rectify any errors or ommisions in future editions.

COVER: © Historic Royal Palaces; David Shurville: 51 (t), 62; Fortean Picture Library: 11 (b), 17, 19, 20, 27, 29, 41, 71, 123, 125, 126, 128, 139; Chris Brackley / Fortean Picture Library: 101; David Binns / Fortean Picture Library: 45; Derek Stafford / Fortean Picture Library: 75; Dr Elmar R. Gruber / Fortean Picture Library: 59; Greg Maxwell / Fortean Picture Library: 120; Karoly Ligeti / Fortean Picture Library; KF Lord / Fortean Picture Library; Paul Vanderhook / Fortean Picture Library: 53; Tony O'Rahilly / Fortean Picture Library: 135; Ghost Research Society: 77; Jude Huff-Felz / Ghost Research Society: 131; © Historic Royal Palaces: 143; Courtesy of Leicester County Museums: 127 (r), 136; Manfred Kage / Science Photo Library: 36 (l); Mary Evans Picture Library: 35; Mary Evans Picture Library / Harry Price Library of Magical Literature: 117; Mary Evans Picture Library / Peter Underwood: 127 (bm), 153; Courtesy of Norah Green: 127 (l), 141; Photography Collections, University of Maryland, Baltimore County: 39; The Society for Psychical Research: 2 (all), 10, 11 (tr), 13, 15, 30, 31 (all), 33, 36 (b), 42, 47, 48, 51 (b), 54, 64, 67, 72, 73 (all), 78, 81, 83, 84, 87, 91, 92, 95, 98, 103, 105, 108, 111, 113, 115, 119, 147; © 2003 Topham Picturepoint: 23; Wm. Becker Collection/American Museum of Photography: 10, 24.